TRAUMA
and
TENACITY
IN VIETNAM

*May this book
bring you closer
to those who
served in Vietnam.
Mary Jane Ingui*

A SURGEON'S STORY

Mary Jane Ingui, PhD

Copyright © 2017 Mary Jane Ingui, PhD
All rights reserved.
No part of this book may be reproduced or transmitted in any form or by
any electronic or mechanical means, including photocopying, recording,
or by any information storage and retrieval system without permission
in writing from the author.

Trauma and Tenacity in Vietnam: A Surgeon's Story is a work of non-fiction.
Any references to real people, events, establishments, organizations, or
locales are accurate as per the recollection, letters and tapes of the subject.

Edited by: Gail Fay gail@faywordworks.com
Book and Cover Design by: Yellow Prelude Design, LLC

ISBN-13: 978-1540895486
ISBN-10: 1540895483

Dedication

I dedicate this book to my husband, Bill Ingui, who has worked tirelessly alongside me to bring this story to the reader; my parents, Josephine and Anthony Capozzoli, and my son, Thomas, who always found time to encourage his mother. I also dedicate this story to the people who have become my family through Dr. Kushner, the MILPHAP team of doctors, nurses and technicians who made survival possible in the city of Vinh Long, Vietnam.

— Mary Jane Ingui, PhD

ABBREVIATIONS

Groups named in this book that are represented by abbreviation letters.

AID.....................Agency for International Development
*United States Government agency which is primarily
responsible for administering civilian foreign aid*

CWCP.............Civilian War Casualty Program
Treatment of civilian casualties in war

DENTCAP.......Dental Civic Action Program
*Dentists and dental technicians with equipment and supplies set up
a temporary field clinic to provide dental treatment to the local population*

MACV............Military Assistance Command Vietnam
*The main American military command unit that had responsibility
for and authority over all U.S. military activities in Vietnam.
Based at Tan Son Nhut.*

MEDCAP.........Medical Civic Action Program
*U.S. medical personnel would go into the villages
to minister to the local populace.*

MILPHAP........Military Provincial Health Assistance Program
*The team of doctors placed into a Vietnamese town or village to improve
the health of Vietnamese civilians; worked under the auspices of MACV*

USMACV.........U.S. Military Assistance Command Vietnam
*Helped in planning hospital construction, medical education
and training, medical supply, public health, and preventative medicine.*

VETCAP...........Veterinarian Civic Action Program
*Veterinarians with equipment and supplies provide limited
veterinarian services for the local population.*

Introduction

In 2011, I was looking for a willing subject for a book. A business professor at Indian River State College in Vero Beach, Florida, suggested I contact Dr. Sheldon Kushner, an adjunct teaching undergraduate anatomy and physiology. We arranged a meeting on campus, and I told him I was a freelance writer currently working for the local paper. Sheldon immediately wanted to talk about the year he spent as a surgeon in Vinh Long, Vietnam. He explained that he had all the letters and audio reel-to-reel tapes he had sent his wife while overseas and that these would tell his story.

Over the next few years, Sheldon showed me these letters. I purchased a vintage 1960s Craig 212 reel-to-reel tape recorder on eBay so I could listen to the audio messages. Sheldon also shared many slides he took with a camera he purchased during a brief visit to Japan. These provided a visual chronicle of his time in country from March 1968 to March 1969.

When we think of Vietnam and medicine, there is a natural tendency to think of the M*A*S*H image of treating American soldiers wounded in combat. However, unlike the TV doctors who helped our servicemen, Sheldon used his medical skills to care for wounded Vietnamese civilians. This role represents a new part of the story that is Vietnam. It was an effort by our government to improve health conditions and showcase America's compassion and good intentions to win the hearts and minds of the South Vietnamese people. Several types of medical units served the South Vietnamese people, and these are detailed in subsequent pages.

The great hope was that the South Vietnamese would embrace these medical practices and continue them, just as our military believed that as we advised the South Vietnamese, they would gain the ability and motivation to defeat the North Vietnamese. This lofty goal of medical mentorship was never achieved, but the men and women who went to do the job came away changed and wholly committed to the idea that they made a difference.

When we read about other people's lives, we feel their triumphs and tragedies; we vicariously experience the lessons life taught them. In Vietnam, Sheldon learned that he was a survivor, a man whose love of medicine was broadened to explore the inner sense of pride in his work. He discovered he had the tenacity to meet the challenge of unrelenting daily surgery and that under less-than-optimal conditions, he and his team could use creativity to accomplish their goal of keeping people alive. His ethics were left intact in spite of what he saw around him.

Most of the letters and tapes utilized in the writing of this book reflect the emotions of an inexperienced 26-year old physician, overwhelmed and unprepared for the horrors of a brutal war that he did not understand. The scars remain imprinted in the minds of many veterans who returned home alive, only to be met by the insensitivity, contempt and hatred conveyed by some people who did not serve in Vietnam and who did not understand.

In the pages ahead, you will see the profound effect Sheldon's service in Vinh Long had on him physically and mentally. It also shaped his opinion on the war. It was truly the defining period of his life.

Mary June Ingui, Ph. D.

Table Of Contents

1

Growing Up in Alabama

McDowell damned me so many times during surgery procedures,
I thought my name was "Damn It" Kushner, not Sheldon Kushner.
He could scream at you for hours and then afterward, take you out for a steak dinner.

Dr. Sheldon Kushner, August 2015

Dr. Sheldon Kushner was born in 1942, a "war baby"[1] and the middle child of Louis and Rose Kushner. He had two brothers: Jack, three years older, and Harold, four years younger. The boys were close growing up and supported each other. They were all good students and all school leaders in high school. Jack was closer in age to Sheldon, and the brothers were later roommates in medical school.

Sheldon and his family lived in a middle-class neighborhood in Montgomery, Alabama. Their house on Felder Avenue had once been occupied by F. Scott Fitzgerald and his wife, Zelda. When Sheldon was three years old, the family moved to National Street in an area called Ridgecrest, an ethnically and religiously mixed neighborhood. He fondly recalled this to be a wonderful blue-collar neighborhood with about 20 boys and a family of four beautiful girls. The neighborhood felt safe; the children would play together in different neighbors' yards under the supervision of the moms, whose authority was never disputed by the other parents. The neighborhood produced four physicians, three lawyers, one judge, one aeronautical engineer, one professional football player, one pharmacist, two teachers, and several business people.

Like many Southern white families, Sheldon's parents hired a black woman to take care of the children. Bertha mainly came to the Kushner home when Rose worked at the family store with her husband. Sheldon has many fond memories of and affection for Bertha. He recalled that "she taught us table manners and how to act in public, especially with adults, [and] it was understood that when she taught us how to behave, it wasn't a request taken lightly; it was a demand."[2] Her affection for him was something he felt deeply.

Rose and Louis Kushner at different times in their lives
(upper right, clockwise; Louis, Jack, Rose, Sheldon and Harold)

While Sheldon's family treated Bertha well and his parents respected the black people who lived in the neighborhood, Montgomery, Alabama, in general experienced racial tension at that time. The city became a hotbed of activity with the rise of the civil rights movement during the late 1940s and early 1950s. "In Montgomery, I saw the black community oppressed in many ways," Sheldon noted. "They had separate water fountains, separate swimming pools, and they had to sit at the back of the bus. It never felt right to me. It saddened me."[3] He added, "You had to be careful about where you went, who you talked to, and what you said in the racially active city of Montgomery."[4]

At five, Sheldon attended Starke University School, a private military school where his brother Jack was two years ahead of him. They wore military uniforms and had to present with shined shoes and brass. The boys were taught to precision march with a wooden rifle. They were taught to have a strict sense of responsibility and follow orders. Sheldon explained, "My parents insisted we address adults with 'Yes, sir/ma'am,' 'No, sir/ma'am.'"[5] When the boys got home after school, their parents insisted that homework be completed before they went out to play. Sheldon believes these values followed him into his later studies in medical school, in the military, and in his career choices.

Sheldon transferred into public school in sixth grade and graduated from Sidney Lanier High School in 1959, where he played football as a linebacker. He was only the second Jewish student to earn a football letter at Lanier. The first was his uncle, Sam Senter, in the late 1920s. During Sheldon's high school years, the Kushner home became a social center for the boys' friends. It was one of the ways Mr. and Mrs. Kushner could monitor their sons' activities and behaviors. Sheldon noted,

> In 2010 we had a reunion of all the children who grew up in our neighborhood on National Street. Almost all who are alive, including Bart [Starr], attended and it was great seeing how so many children from this blue-collar neighborhood did so well in life.[6]

As a young boy, Sheldon attended a reformed temple in Montgomery, but when he was 11, his family changed to a conservative synagogue, which better suited their religious and political convictions. The weekend included Saturday services and Sunday school for education in his faith. Sheldon finished his Hebrew studies, which were scheduled so they didn't interfere with his football practice, and made his Bar Mitzvah at 13. All of his Christian friends were invited to attend.

When the Kushners lived on National Avenue, their closest friends in the neighborhood were Bryan, a sergeant in the U.S. Air Force, and Lula Starr. The families played canasta three times a week, and every Christmas, Mrs. Starr would walk across the street to deliver her heavenly hash for the Kushners to enjoy.

Lanier Defensive End Star, Sheldon Kushner, posing for the local newspaper

Bryan and Lula's son Bart was about eight years older than Sheldon and frequently babysat for Sheldon and his brothers when their parents went out. Bart was a good student and often helped Sheldon with his homework. He also played football at Lanier High School, and when Sheldon began to play, Bart taught him how to block and tackle and how to pass and catch the football.

Bart Starr went on to make a name for himself as a star quarterback at the University of Alabama and then as an All-Pro quarterback with the Green Bay Packers (1956–1971). He played in the first two Super Bowls and later became a member of the Pro Football Hall of Fame. After his playing days ended, Bart became the head coach for the Green Bay Packers from 1975 to 1983. When Bart was playing football at the University of Alabama, Bart's parents often took Sheldon and his older brother, Jack, to Tuscaloosa or Birmingham to see Bart play. Bart and Sheldon have remained lifelong friends.

Bart Starr, Quarterback for the Green Bay Packers

Retired, during a speaking engagement

During the 1950s, Sheldon's uncle, Eugene Feldman, his mother's brother, was writing controversial articles for the *Montgomery Adviser*, criticizing the practice of racial segregation. His articles resulted in threats against Sheldon's extended family. Sheldon did not understand at the time that because Eugene was Jewish and gay, he was a big target for violent discrimination. Eugene also played a role in the famous story of Rosa Parks.

On December 1, 1955, Rosa Parks, a 42-year-old African American seamstress, refused to give up her seat to a white man while riding on a city bus in Montgomery, Alabama. For doing this, Rosa Parks was arrested and fined for breaking the laws of segregation. Sheldon's uncle Eugene, along with the Smith and Durr families,[7] provided bail for Rosa Parks when she was jailed. Rosa Parks's refusal to leave her seat sparked the Montgomery Bus Boycott and is considered the beginning of the modern civil rights movement.[8]

It was after that event that Eugene left Montgomery. The circumstances are unclear but worth noting. Sheldon's older brother, Jack, contends that:

> Joe Azbell, of the *Montgomery Advertiser*, called my father and mother, and told them that Eugene had written some articles and that Eugene was causing a problem. He then said that the KKK was threatening to kill him [Eugene]. He advised my parents to arm the family and advised them to get Eugene out of town or he will get killed. My father and mother became frightened, and Eugene voluntarily left town in order to avoiding getting killed.[9]

Sheldon's younger brother Harold, believes, "My parents forced Eugene out of town and it is a shameful part of our history. They should never have done that. What people of courage do is stand up to problems."[10] Sheldon explained, "My parents were looking out for the family; they wanted to protect their children no matter which version of the story you want to accept."[11] Thinking about the role that Joe Azbell played in his family, Sheldon said, "He did us a favor and became close friends with my parents. Later he became a speech writer for George Wallace, when he ran for governor and later, for president."[12]

After Uncle Eugene left Montgomery, he lived in South Carolina for a short time before moving to Chicago to attend the University of Chicago, where he received a PhD in political science. He spent the rest of his life supporting black causes and was alienated from the rest of his family. He later became one of the founders of the DuSable Museum of African American History.[13] Sheldon corresponded with Eugene many years later when he was doing his residency at the University of Cincinnati and through their correspondence got better acquainted with his uncle. Eugene even visited him in Cincinnati.

The DuSable Museum of African American History,
located in Chicago, Illinois

PHOTO CREDIT © ANTONIO VERNON

Sheldon noted that since all their extended family members were Jewish, they too were targets. When he was about six or seven, one of the boys in the neighborhood called Sheldon a "dirty Jew." "I had no idea what that meant, and my parents did not dwell on it at the time," he said.[14] His friends were both Jews and Christians.

Sheldon's parents' grocery store, the ABC Market, was located in a black area of Montgomery. Quite the entrepreneurs, they also owned three cafes, one of which served food and liquor and was connected to the grocery store. The other cafes were named Bob and Jack's Grill (named after Sheldon Robert Kushner and Jack Kushner) and Harold's Grill, named after Sheldon's younger brother. With the income generated from these businesses, the Kushners sent Sheldon and his two brothers to college and graduate school. After their undergraduate studies, Sheldon and Jack both attended the University of Alabama Medical School, while Harold attended law school. Sheldon's parents were also able to purchase several duplexes and freestanding homes.

Sheldon attended college at the University of Alabama in Tuscaloosa, where he was a premed major. He graduated in 1963. It was here that he first experienced religious discrimination. This hurt, but it gave him insight into how the black population felt in those days. He explained that Jews were not allowed to be in fraternities that only allowed Christians. So, he joined a Jewish fraternity, ZBT (Zeta Beta Tau), on campus and made several lifelong friends.

When Sheldon applied to various medical schools, he discovered that each one had Jewish quotas. They would only admit a set number of Jewish applicants. He settled on the University of Alabama and stayed there for his internship as well, graduating with his MD in 1966. The internship (1966–1967) required that he serve in different areas of medicine— such as obstetrics, internal medicine, and the emergency room. Many of the patients who received treatment from Sheldon during his medical school days were black. There were "Colored" and "White" medical wards. Sheldon recalled,

> I didn't like the situation but I couldn't do anything about it. Throughout my time in medical school and internship in Birmingham (during the 1960s), I experienced the tragedy of the little girls murdered when the church was blown up. I experienced the race riots and the people brought into the emergency room with injuries from dogs, water cannons, and billy clubs. It was ugly, it was so wrong, and I hated it and my heart went out to these unfortunate people who were subjected to this hatred.[15]

Although medical school was rigorous and exhausting, Sheldon had the opportunity to work with several renowned medical professors. One example was Dr. Tinsley Harrison, who was the author of a textbook that became the bible for internal medicine, according to Sheldon. The head of all surgery at the medical school was Dr. Champ Lyons, who was trained at Tulane University, the same school where Dr. Michael E. DeBakey, the world-renowned pioneer in heart surgery, was trained. DeBakey was the chancellor emeritus of Baylor College of Medicine in Houston, Texas; director of the Methodist DeBakey Heart and Vascular Center; and senior attending surgeon of the Methodist Hospital in Houston. He is known for his work on the treatment of heart patients and for his role in the development of the mobile army surgical hospital.[16]

Sheldon recalled the culture and climate of medical school under Dr. Lyons' supervision:

Dr. Champ Lyons

> While I was a junior medical student, I went to the hospital one day, at eight o'clock that night, to do an appendectomy with the resident, Dan Merck. We were scrubbing at the scrub basin, and coming from the end of the hall, I heard, "You dumb son-of-a-bitch, you dumb son-of-a-bitch, you bastard!" I said, "What is that?" Merck responded by saying, "Oh, that's just Dr. Lyons teaching!"[17]

Sheldon's favorite professor was Dr. Holt McDowell, whom students called "Captain Midnight." Sheldon explained, "McDowell would show up at midnight for rounds, starting with a ton of coffee and cigarettes in the cafeteria." It was an interesting experience working with Dr. McDowell. Sheldon describes wondering about his own name: "McDowell damned me so many times during surgery procedures, I thought my name was 'Damn It' Kushner, not Sheldon Kushner. He could scream at you for hours and then afterward, take you out for a steak dinner."[18] Holt McDowell was trained by Dr. Champ Lyons and may have picked up some of his habits. It was trial by fire for medical students in those days.

Sheldon related another story about Champ Lyons:

> I remember Dr. Lyons used to make rounds with the residents every Tuesday morning. Medical students weren't allowed, but we became useful. It was an ass-chewing session. Lyons would raise hell about everything. So what the chief residents used to do, if they had a patient that was going to be a problem and they were going to get chewed out by him, they would ask us, the medical students, to take the patient up to a room on the 14th floor, later calling us to bring him or her back, or we would put the patient on the elevator, going up and down, until the rounds were over.[19]

Over time, medical school students honed their survival skills.

Years later, Sheldon met Dr. Phil Morgan, who was a surgeon in Vero Beach, Florida, and who had also trained under Dr. Lyons. To this day, Morgan is frightened when he wakes up on Tuesday mornings, thinking about rounds with Champ. Sheldon remarked, "That's how surgery was taught then, but if you talked to a student like that today, you probably would get sued."[20]

When Dr. Lyons passed away in 1965, Dr. John Kirkland, chairman of heart surgery at the Mayo Clinic in Rochester, Minnesota, replaced him. Sheldon describes the scene when Kirkland had to decide whether he wanted the position at the University of Alabama Medical School in Birmingham. He visited the medical school when Sheldon was an intern. Sheldon recalled this event at the school:

When Dr. Kirkland arrived on a Saturday morning to do rounds with us, the chief resident was Hansel Peacock, who presented patients to Dr. Kirkland. He said, "Dr. Kirkland, this patient is about 24-hours post-op gunshot wound to the abdomen; this patient is about 6-hours post-op with a wound to the chest and to the abdomen; this patient is about 8-hours post-op gunshot wound to the chest." Dr. Kirkland interrupted, "Wait a minute, you guys seem like you handle trauma well, but do you have any thyroid cases?" "Oh yes sir," replied Peacock. "This patient is two days post-op gunshot wound to the thyroid." And it was true! We had a gunshot wound to everything. This was Alabama, man, and I was ready for Vietnam. At the time it wasn't funny, but to look back on it now, it was pretty funny.[21]

During high school and during breaks at college and medical school, Sheldon went back home and often helped his dad in the grocery store. His dad had hired a young black man named Johnny Adams to help at the store; later, Sheldon's dad taught Johnny to be a butcher. Over the years, Sheldon and Johnny carried many grocery boxes and slabs of meat for the store. Sheldon explained, "When I was working in the store, I did pretty much everything. I clerked, cleaned, and learned how to butcher meat." Johnny passed on the butchering expertise, and he became Sheldon's friend. Sheldon laughed about how they would compete to see who could lift more groceries and meat; this lifting helped him keep in shape for football.[22] When Sheldon's dad retired, he deeded the property and the store to Johnny, who by that time had a wife and family.

The store also became a gathering place for all of Sheldon's friends and a place where he met some very interesting people. For about a six-month period, a young white woman named Mary Jo Kopechne occasionally visited his father's store. The first time she came in she was with two black men. Kopechne was in Montgomery to teach for a year at the Mission of St. Jude, an activity that was part of the civil rights movement. She came into the store many times to purchase writing tablets and pencils. Sheldon's dad talked with her whenever she came in and asked her about her family. "The more he got to know her, the more he liked her," Sheldon said. Years later he was very upset when he learned she was killed on the evening of July 18, 1969, while riding in an Oldsmobile with Ted Kennedy; the car fell into Poucha Pond, overturning in the water. Kennedy extracted himself from the vehicle, but Kopechne did not survive.[23]

Sheldon's years growing up in Montgomery formed the backdrop to his life-changing experience in Vietnam. Through the friendships formed in his close-knit neighborhood and through working at his parents' store, Sheldon learned to interact and empathize with all kinds of people. He also learned tenacity as he worked toward and achieved the goal of attending medical school. Empathy and tenacity served Sheldon well in treating civilian casualties in Vinh Long.

2

Arrival in Vietnam: First Impressions

Saigon is a most amazing place. I was immediately overwhelmed by the filth,
the smell, the crowded conditions, and the traffic. . . . The Vietnamese are very nice people,
but they can really frustrate the hell out of you.

Captain Sheldon Kushner, MD, March 1968

During the 1960s, under President Kennedy and President Johnson, there was an increase in the American military presence in South Vietnam. Because of the war in Vietnam, Sheldon was notified that he would have to serve in the military when he finished his internship in 1967. Under the Armed Forces Physician Appointment and Residency Consideration Program, or the Berry Plan,[24] young doctors could go into the military either after their internship, after one year of residency, or after completion of residency. Sheldon had already been accepted to an OB-GYN residency that was set to begin after his internship; however, the U.S. government intervened and he was forced to join the U.S. Air Force before his residency began.[25]

Initially, in September 1967, Sheldon went into the Air Force and was sent for basic training to Shepherd Air Force Base near Wichita Falls, Texas. He recalled, "Part of the training involved mock mass casualty exercises. I also learned some of the mundane things like how to wear a uniform, put on the shiny buttons, and salute. None of it seemed very real."[26] Then he was stationed at Vandenberg Air Force Base just north of Santa Barbara, California, where he served as a general medical officer. Sheldon enjoyed the climate and was happy with this position. It was late in 1967, just before the Tet Offensive,[27] when Dr. Sheldon Kushner was told he was going to Vietnam. Sheldon's older brother, Jack, had just returned from Vietnam where he, too, had served as a general surgeon.

Before being sent overseas, Sheldon married his girlfriend, Carol, a registered nurse working on the internal medicine floor at University Hospital in Birmingham, Alabama; Sheldon and Carol met while he was an intern at the same hospital. After getting engaged

Dr. Sheldon Kushner, surgeon, US Air Force,
age 26, shortly after arriving in Vinh Long, Vietnam.

in the spring of 1967, she came out to California in November of 1967, where they were married by a rabbi at the Jewish synagogue in Santa Barbara, California. Ten of the doctors at Vandenberg Air Force Base and their families attended their wedding and dinner afterward. None of the bride's or groom's relatives attended the ceremony.

Sheldon was then sent to Brook Army Hospital in San Antonio, Texas, for two weeks to attend a crash course in tropical diseases. During these sessions, they discussed snakebites and malaria. As it turned out, Sheldon never encountered these things in Vietnam, although everyone had to take a prophylaxis or a combination of medicines to prevent disease, in this case, malaria. The medicines included Primaquine (or Primaquine Phosphate), a medication used in the treatment of malaria, as well as Chloroquine (also known as Chloroquine Phosphate), an antimalarial medicine. They are available in the United States by prescription only.

Upon his return to Vandenberg following the crash course, Sheldon was granted a 30-day leave to visit home in Montgomery, Alabama. While he was home, the newlyweds located an apartment for Carol, who was still employed at University Hospital in Birmingham.

After receiving all of the standard shots and malaria pills needed to go overseas, Sheldon received orders that he was assigned to Tan Son Nhut Air Force Base[28] near Saigon, Vietnam, and would be reporting for duty there in March of 1968. In a reel-to-reel tape he later sent his wife, Sheldon recounted that on March 18, 1968, he boarded a Pan American plane at Travis Air Force Base near Sacramento, California. It was a commercial flight contracted by the government. All those on board were bound for Vietnam. A preacher got on the plane and said a prayer, which ended with this admonition: "I wish you all the best, but it's unfortunate that I tell you that you need to look at the person on your right and the person on your left 'cause one of you won't be coming back."[29] The plane stopped in Hawaii, in Guam, and in the Philippines. Its final destination was Saigon.

South Vietnam, with Vinh Long City southwest of Saigon
(center of map) near the Mekong Delta, the thriving rice bowl of Southeast Asia

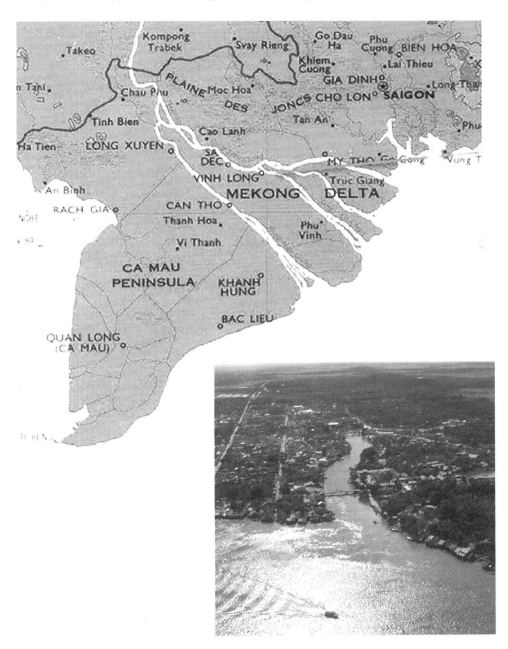

Vinh Long City from the vantage point
of a Cessna L-19 Bull Dog

Street Photo: Common city scene in downtown Vinh Long

Before he left for Vietnam, Sheldon received a letter from a doctor in Vinh Long, explaining that Sheldon would be taking his job in that city. Sheldon said, "When I received the letter, I didn't pay much attention to it because my orders said I was going to Tan Son Nhut. It couldn't be right. I learned that it was exactly what was to happen shortly after arriving at the air base in March."[30]

Captain Sheldon Kushner arrived in Tan Son Nhut Air Force Base in March of 1968. This was about two months after the Tet Offensive. By 1968, 525,000 American troops were in South Vietnam.[31] On February 1968, the U.S. State Department announced the highest U.S. casualty toll of the Vietnam War. During the previous week, 543 Americans were killed in action, and 2,547 had been wounded. By March, Senator Robert Kennedy announced that he would be running for president, and President Johnson delivered an address to the nation in which he announced steps to limit the war in Vietnam. He also surprised many by stating he would not seek reelection as president. By April of 1968, Defense Secretary Clark Clifford announced a new troop ceiling of 549,500 American soldiers in Vietnam. In reality, the total number of Americans in country peaked at 541,000 by August 1968.

When he reported for duty, Sheldon was told he would be part of the Military Assistance Command Vietnam (MACV). For his service, he would receive $400 per month, of which he kept $30 for his personal needs and sent the rest to Carol. When he picked up his equipment—which included three sets of jungle fatigues, two pairs of nylon jungle boots, a .45 pistol, and outdoor cooking gear—he questioned why he needed such gear. He learned these were all standard issue of the Army. Captain Sheldon Kushner, U.S. Air Force,

Areal Photo: River crossroads in Vinh Long

was now on loan to the Army. He would be stationed in the Mekong Delta in a place called Vinh Long province located about 60 miles south of Saigon. Sheldon was going to be part of the Military Provincial Health Assistance Program (MILPHAP).

Sheldon attended a three-day orientation at a MACV hotel compound in Saigon where he was taught some Vietnamese words and phrases along with some cultural dos and don'ts about how to talk to the Vietnamese people. He would later learn how Vietnamese culture would affect the medical treatment he and the MILPHAP team provided the civilians.

Sheldon summarized his first days in country in a letter to his wife Carol dated March 22, 1968:

> Saigon is a most amazing place. I was immediately overwhelmed by the filth, the smell, the crowded conditions, the traffic (this is unbelievable). The heat and humidity are fierce, but not intolerable as yet as it does cool off at night. I am definitely going to Vinh Long unless something is changed in the next 3 days. From all I can gather, this has been a relatively safe place so far. I certainly hope that it remains so. I am now in a MACV hotel compound in Saigon. I will stay here for about three days after which I will go on down to Vinh Long. I spent my first night here at Tan Son Nhut AFB. The base was hit heavily with mortar fire but I never heard a sound, as I was so sound asleep. Last night I took my first shower since leaving San Francisco and my second shave. I felt like someone had given me a million dollars.[32]

A day later, while at MACV headquarters before leaving for Vinh Long, Sheldon wrote, "I am still getting briefings here, some comforting and some very disturbing, but all and all I am doing fine, maybe a little scared, but otherwise OK."[33] After six days in country, he went to the airport at the base near Saigon to get a flight to Vinh Long, the capital of Vinh Long province. He boarded a C-123 that was used for transporting supplies and people. After a one-hour flight, he landed at the Army airfield in Vinh Long and hitched a ride in a Jeep to the MACV compound, a five-minute drive.

A corner building destroyed in Vinh Long where Sheldon was stationed

Sheldon's MILPHAP team worked under the auspices of the MACV; the 9th Army Division was the only division in this area of Vietnam. It was estimated that about 6,000 Viet Cong troops were operating in Vinh Long Province. Sheldon and his team lived in an old Vietnamese hotel built by the French that had been taken over by the Army and made into an American compound. It had its own kitchen, providing meals for them. American compound personnel and Vietnamese guards protected its inhabitants.

The city of Vinh Long, a town of about 30,000 to 40,000 people, was the province headquarters, about five miles away from a U.S. Army airstrip. Everywhere Sheldon drove, the streets were filled with bicycles, street markets and images of the war. The center of the town featured a tall obelisk and closer to the hospital, there were several buildings partly destroyed sometime during the conflict.

Heavy bike traffic along the main street in Vinh Long

Obelisk in the center of the main street, Vinh Long

Visions from the Streets of Vinh Long

Using measuring cups, this child is
selling rice to local customers

Very common scene of a
busy marketplace in Vinh Long

Family selling unrefrigerated meat in the open air

Crocks of Nuoc Mam Cham (Dipping Fish Sauce)

Several older citizens would be seen on the street.
Note the soiled scarf, straw hat by his side and sandals

The Mekong River was nearby, which was used as a bathroom, bathtub, and washing machine and, of course, as a means of transportation by the Vietnamese. Approximately 485,000 people lived in Vinh Long Province.[34] Vinh Long was located between the Mekong and Bassac Rivers. Before Sheldon had arrived in Vinh Long, it was determined by the U.S. and Vietnamese militaries that easy access to and flow of rice through this area was vital. Since the Viet Cong controlled the area as early as 1963–1964, the rice traffic had to make a long detour to Long Xuyen Province, near the Cambodian border. Then the rice would need to move south again and unload at a site across the Mekong River from the city of Vinh Long. From there, the rice was transported by trucks to Saigon and Cho Long. In his book The Twenty-Five Year Century, General Lam Quang Thi explained, "It was estimated that the reopening of the Mang Thit-Nicolai canal would save two and a half days travel time for Siagon-bound rice traffic; this would constitute a tremendous boost to the local economy."[35]

The 30-mile Mang Thit-Nicolai canal was designed at the turn of the century by a French engineer named Nicolai. With the countryside filled with wet rice paddies and dotted with palm trees, the area was the rice bowl of Vietnam.[36] During the time when Sheldon was in Vietnam, the area of the Mekong Delta produced 4,202,400 tons of rice in 1968.[37] Control of the province was vital to the economy.

Freshly planted rice fields

This was the environment that Sheldon would immerse himself. He was in the heart of the rice bowl and the everyday people he observed became his patients. In March 1968, Sheldon became a new addition to the MILPHAP team in Vinh Long, where his practice of medicine would be tested time and again as the United States attempted to maintain control of this vital area during the war.

Farmers tending the fields, planting the rice; note the protective hats from the sun

Rice in full growth before harvesting

3

The Medical Team

Surgery, surgery, surgery all day, every day. You know it can really get old.

Captain Sheldon Kushner, MD, September 1968

A modern science-based, nationwide health-care system did not exist in the 1960s in South Vietnam. According to Robert J. Wilensky, writing about medicine for Vietnamese civilians, South Vietnam had only 1,400 doctors during the 1960s, and 1,000 of them were in its army. The 400 civilian physicians were generally located in the major cities to care for 16 million civilians.[38]

Wilensky writes that the U.S. government funded various types of health-care programs for the Vietnamese during the war. A primary care traveling program was called Medical Civic Action Program (MEDCAP). U.S. dental and veterinary military personnel were also part of this program. Under the Dental Civic Action Program (DENTCAP), dental officers and enlisted technicians provided dental treatments to the Vietnamese. Under VETCAP (Veterinarian Civic Action Program), U.S. Army veterinary personnel treated sick and wounded animals, provided cattle vaccinations, and gave advice in the feeding and care of cattle and swine. A program to care for Vietnamese war-related injuries was called Civilian War Casualty Program (CWCP), and a hospital-based program to train and deliver more sophisticated care was named Military Provincial Health Assistance Program (MILPHAP).[39] Sheldon was part of the MILPHAP team in Vinh Long, Vietnam.

The United States' MILPHAP was created by the Agency for International Development (AID) and the U.S. Military Assistance Command Vietnam (USMACV) to improve the health of Vietnamese civilians. The U.S. Secretary of Defense directed the services to develop this program in 1965.[40] In November of that year, one team had been established. By May of 1968, there were eight Army, seven Navy, and seven Air Force MILPHAP teams. By 1970, teams existed in 25 of Vietnam's 44 provinces.[41]

MILPHAP Team Photo; Shown in khaki uniform to the left are
Fred Seaman, Sheldon Kushner and their Vietnamese doctor counterpart,
Basci Gian, who will prove troubling to some of the American doctors

Each MILPHAP team consisted of three doctors, one medical administrative officer, and 12 enlisted technicians. The team was assigned to a Vietnamese provincial hospital and under the supervision of a provincial chief of medicine. These teams provided clinical, medical, and surgical care and supported local public health programs.

The major purpose of the team was to develop an independent, self-sustaining health service program in South Vietnam. To meet this objective, the team had to focus on improving the medical skills of the Vietnamese. More specifically, the mission was to provide medical care and health services to Vietnamese civilians, develop the surgical skills of Vietnamese doctors, and train hospital staff workers.[42] In 1970, over 700 Vietnamese nurses received training in hospitals supported by MILPHAP teams.[43]

Along with the creation of MILPHAP teams, a medical policy coordinating committee was established in 1965 to plan and organize the medical programs providing aid to Vietnamese civilians. By 1968, joint USMACV and AID committees were created to eliminate duplication of civilian health programs. These committees included military and civilian Vietnamese medical officials along with USMACV personnel in planning hospital construction, medical education and training, medical supply, public health, and preventative medicine. As with our military role in South Vietnam, the role of the U.S. doctors was temporary; in the future, it was assumed, the South Vietnamese would be solely responsible for these programs.[44] It never happened.

MILPHAP compound and living quarters from a distance

Entrance to the MILPHAP compound

MILPHAP compound shown from inside the unit toward the street and the guardhouse

MILPHAP compound to the left, looking down the street

In addition to MILPHAP, the Volunteer Physicians for Vietnam program brought volunteer civilian doctors to Vietnam to work with the MILPHAP team. From 1966 to 1973, the American Medical Association administered Volunteer Physicians for Vietnam, an effort that sent U.S. physicians to war-torn Vietnam to provide medical care to civilians for 60-, 90-, or 120-day tours.[45] They lived in their own compound downtown and paid South Vietnamese guards to protect them. Likewise, nurses who volunteered lived in a house that was within walking distance from the MILPHAP compound and were guarded by Vietnamese soldiers.

Sheldon's MILPHAP team (Unit 558)—which consisted of three doctors, about 10 medical corpsmen, Army Special Forces, Green Berets, Air Force Forward Air Control people, and CIA civilian types (who advised the Vietnamese in covert activities)—lived in the old French hotel. Sheldon noted, "Vietnamese housekeepers washed our clothes and cleaned our rooms."[46] Some Vietnamese women tended the bar at the top of the compound building where soldiers drank, played cards, and viewed movies, when available. One of the CIA civilians Sheldon got to know was Don Ackerman, who worked as a border patrol agent in Texas and was a musician in the El Paso Symphony Orchestra. He was an adviser to the national police in Vinh Long and was assigned to teach the South Vietnamese about terrorism. In all, there were about 160 people living in this compound.

This living facility was not absolutely secure. There were American guards posted at all times throughout the compound. They shared this responsibility with Vietnamese guards as well. Sheldon explained, "We lived in a very dangerous area. Nothing was completely secure, which is why we had to have guards."[47] They had to worry about people on motorcycles who would ride past the MILPHAP compound and throw explosives at the guards. There were several such incidents during Sheldon's tour of duty.[48]

Sheldon soon discovered that his internship had provided only minimal preparation for his life as a trauma surgeon. From the beginning, Sheldon's role as a physician in Vinh Long, South Vietnam, was not the typical one. His job was to care for injured Vietnamese civilians in a 400-bed civilian hospital, an old building built by the French. The hospital was located in the middle of the downtown area of Vinh Long.

On Sheldon's first day, the doctors explained his duties and responsibilities and took him to the hospital to meet his Vietnamese counterpart, Bacsi Gian, a doctor in his mid-40s who had been trained by the French. One duty of the team was to train Vietnamese doctors, but there was only one in the hospital, Bacsi Gian. This doctor rejected any training by Americans and often engaged in unethical practices, as well as medical practices that were substandard to those practiced in the United States and were foreign to Sheldon and his colleagues. Other personnel included three Vietnamese translators, two women and one man, who helped the doctors understand the patients' needs.

Although the MILPHAP team primarily provided medical care to the civilian population injured by the war, the team occasionally treated minor medical problems of the American personnel living in the compound. The American personnel in the area were mainly treated at the Army airfield nearby, or they were sent by helicopter to an American field hospital outside of Vinh Long, where they could be treated by American physicians, including many specialists. From there some were transported to an American hospital in Japan. Injured Vietnamese civilians were treated by the MILPHAP team in Vinh Long and could not be transferred anywhere.

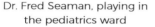

Dr. Fred Seaman, playing in
the pediatrics ward

Nurse Jackie Ventura working with an injured
child, alongside the child's father

Three doctors served at this facility. One of the doctors Sheldon worked with was Fred Seaman, a board-certified pediatrician in his late 20s. According to Sheldon, Fred rarely performed surgery. Instead, he provided care to the Vietnamese children who were sick or post-op, and he also served as commander of the MILPHAP team.[49] The other doctor was James Gordon "Mac" McComb,[50] also in his late 20s and a graduate from RPI (Rensselaer Polytechnic Institute) in New York State.

None of these men had extensive experience with surgery, yet they were expected to operate on abdomens, brains, blood vessels, and more. They also did many skin grafts because of napalm burns.

Assisting these three doctors were two civilian nurses, who were in Vietnam for an eighteen-month training program, and ten medical corpsmen; the whole team shared the care of the patients following surgery. One of the nurses, Marcella O'Connor, took care of the operating room. She kept up with supplies and equipment, ordering whatever was needed, and taught the Vietnamese how to sterilize medical instruments and package and store equipment.

The other nurse, Jackie Ventura, took care of post-operative children and other sick children in the Pediatric Unit and worked closely with Fred Seaman.

The corpsmen assisted in surgery, sutured small lacerations, did minor debridement of wounds, irrigated post-op wounds, set broken bones in casts, and changed dressings when needed.[51]

Finally, a husband and wife team—Ong Thoai, whom they called Charlie Brown, an X-ray technician for the hospital, and his wife, Ba (Mrs.) Houng, the head nurse—were invaluable additions to Sheldon and his colleagues. Ba Houng was in charge of the male post-op surgical unit, working closely with Sheldon, who was in charge of male surgery. Her husband assisted in surgery, did minor procedures, and performed cast work and whatever else had to be done. In addition, Mac, who was in charge of female surgery, worked closely with Ba Tam, who was the head nurse on the female post-op unit.

Husband and wife. Ong (Mr.) Thoai [also known as Charlie Brown] and Ba (Mrs.) Houng

Nurses Co Sa and Co Thuan

Ba-Tam, Head Surgical Nurse

Sheldon with Ong Thoai and Ba Houng

Next door to the hospital was an orphanage run by Irish Catholic nuns. One of the sisters, when she had time, would come over to the hospital and help the team care for the patients. There was also another orphanage in Vinh Long run by Vietnamese nuns.

Vietnam became a country of orphans because over the years of war, parents were killed and children had no other family to care for them. Outside on the streets of Vinh Long, a cadre of little orphan children would often meet Sheldon and the others.

Their smiling faces masked the realities of the war that surrounded them. It was a mission of hope the doctors brought, and the children were a bright part of Sheldon's tour.

Sister from the orphanage down the street from Vinh Long Hospital who would work with doctors and patients

Orphanage nearby the Hospital

Faces of the Orphans

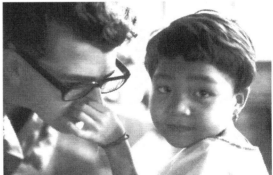

Orphan girl being entertained
by Corpsman Tom Graue

The Volunteer Physicians in Vietnam program provided several American civilian physicians for about three months at a time to assist Sheldon and his team. Ray Brewer, an ophthalmologist from Houston, was one of them. Loren Morgan, an ophthalmologist from Wyoming, was another. These doctors lived in their own compound and paid South Vietnamese to guard them. Loren and Ray's expertise was needed, as Tom Graue, a medic who worked with Ray and the other civilian physicians, noted that "removal of the eyeball was the most frequent surgery performed by these doctors."[52] In addition, they performed cataract surgery on a population that had never seen eye doctors.[53]

A clinic outside the hospital, staffed with Vietnamese doctors, treated the day-to-day medical needs of the Vietnamese. In contrast, the MILPHAP group and civilian volunteer doctors and nurses took care of the civilian war casualties.

With Mac and Fred, and the medics and other staff mentioned earlier, Sheldon embarked on his one-year tour of duty at Vinh Long City Hospital.

Vinh Long Hospital Entrance

Courtyard and waiting area of the hospital

Courtyard from another angle

Food was prepared in this kitchen for patients and family members

The hospital Outpatient building

The TB (Tuberculosis) Ward

The MILPHAP in Action

I am doing 2 to 3 to 4 major op cases a day and many, many minor procedures.
This afternoon, they brought in 14 9-year-old kids, whose school was blown up,
seven were dead and 1 died shortly. A sadder sight I don't believe I have ever seen.
I just wish I knew more and that I could do more for these kids.

Captain Sheldon Kushner, MD, May 1968

Sheldon settled into his new environment with the MILPHAP team, and within a few days he was performing multiple daily surgeries at Vinh Long Hospital. On March 30, 1968, he wrote to his wife about working with the locals. His impressions reflected those of many other servicemen and women stationed in Vietnam:

> The Vietnamese are very nice people, but they can really frustrate the hell out of you. They are a somewhat lazy people. Their lunch break every day is from 12:00 noon until 2:30 p.m. They usually start late and quit early. They do not want you to advise them (which is what we are supposed to be doing), they want you to do the work for them and they want you to do it their way. Can you imagine that?? If ever there was a group of people who needed to be industrious it is this group. Charlie or the V.C., are well trained and hard working. If we were to leave, this place would belong to Charlie over night.[54]

Despite the rough conditions, minimal supplies, lack of help, and local customs, Sheldon and his colleagues embraced the Hippocratic Oath. They practiced medicine by serving the patient to the best of their ability. Sheldon's letters to his wife reveal his deep concerns about his ability to serve his patients and the devastating effects the war had on those civilians in Vinh Long. Sheldon was determined to master his profession, although he was often frustrated by the experience of working with the locals and with performing

Sheldon near the jeep he rode to the hospital

surgeries that were often unfamiliar to the team. He and his team relied on tenacity and creativity to help their patients survive. He attributed such qualities to his internship experience in Birmingham, Alabama. Sheldon remarked, "Given the environment in the Deep South at that time, I learned the importance of tenacity in dealing with adverse situations."[55] The real challenge was not knowing enough and wanting to do more for his patients. In short, the conditions of war created opportunities for ingenuity and practicality.

Sheldon and his colleague Mac were expected to perform a wide range of surgical procedures involving virtually every part of the human body, even though neither of them had extensive surgical experience before coming to the hospital in Vinh Long. Each brought his own medical experiences to the circumstances that existed for them in Vinh Long, and together they devised "medical protocols" that they believed would work best for their patients, saving lives and limbs under almost impossible conditions that were unlike those found in the pristine environment of American hospitals and clinics. Practicing medicine in Vinh Long meant treating injuries rarely or never seen during Sheldon's days at the University of Alabama Medical School.

Each morning Sheldon traveled by jeep from the protected compound to Vinh Long City Hospital to begin work.

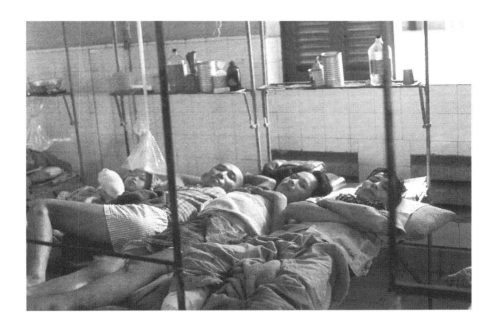

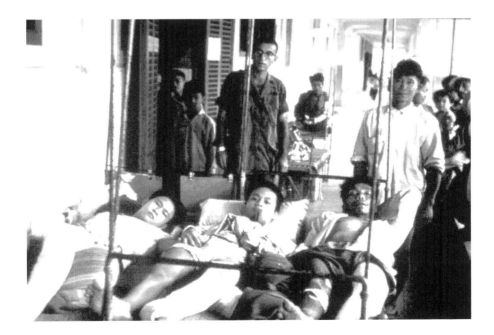

Crowded beds with patients; Dr. Kushner standing behind the group

Useless supplies piled on the Vinh Long Hospital porch

On most days, there were about 30 to 40 patients in the hospital needing care. The innocent civilians' injuries resulted from bombings, small fire arms, rocket fire, mortars, claymore mine explosions, booby trap explosions, and napalm burns at the hands of the Viet Cong guerrillas, the Americans, and the South Vietnamese Army; there were no North Vietnamese regulars in that province, only Viet Cong.[56] In one of his many letters to his wife, Sheldon described the scene:

> I walked into the hospital this morning and found 41 new war casualties. Where in the hell do you start? I did 5 major cases, Fred Seaman did 2 and we still have many left. This was all the result of a mortar attack last night. Would you believe that I did a saphenous vein graft to repair a cut axillary artery? I don't know if it will work, but I tried. Only time will tell.[57]

Each morning the three doctors would triage and decide which civilians could be helped. This methodology was also applied in other hospital and combat areas in Vietnam. This meant that patients were separated into groups: those who could survive without immediate treatment, those who could survive if their wounds were treated immediately, and sadly, those who were so severely injured that they would most likely die despite treatment. Having set these protocols, the doctors addressed staffing next. Under triage conditions, Sheldon said, "medical assignments were loose; you put people where they were needed when you came in that day."[58]

Their work day usually lasted 12 hours, until about 6 or 7 p.m. Because the area was only protected by the U.S. Army during the day, Sheldon's team did not work at night. The injured coming to the hospital at night had to wait until the next morning or be treated by the Vietnamese on staff during the night.

There were three operating rooms; each could accommodate about three patients at a time. The Seabees, Navy enlisted men, built these operating facilities before Sheldon arrived in Vietnam.

The staff could never help everyone in a given day because a new wave of people would come in each morning; no new doctors or nurses were added to the unit during Sheldon's tour, which could have lightened the work load. "There was never any catching up,"[59] he remarked. In the hospital ward itself, beds were made of straw mats. Two beds were put together so four or five patients could rest after surgery. Such crowded conditions were the norm, as were those 12-hour days.

Since their hospital facility was at the bottom of the supply chain, they often had to wait for medical supplies. In addition, there was always a need for intravenous fluids. They had the standard operating tools that Sheldon said were adequate at best. On occasion the hospital would receive useless supplies, such as dextrose, that would be piled up outside.

Although most of his work in Vinh Long involved performing various types of surgeries, Sheldon had other responsibilities. Treating sexually transmitted diseases took Sheldon away from his heavy schedule of surgery. On April 4, 1968, the day Martin Luther King was assassinated in Memphis, Tennessee, Sheldon wrote to his wife:

> You will never believe what I am doing now. The colonel has decided that there are too many GIs in the area with Gonorrhea. So, he has selected yours truly to run a special clinic for all the Vietnamese prostitutes to try to eliminate the disease as much as possible. So one day I can tell our children that their daddy went to war in Vietnam to fight the G.C. while everyone else was fighting the V.C.[60]

Fifteen days later, on April 19, 1968, Sheldon updated his wife on his progress: "My V.D. clinic is running right along, but I really don't know how much good I am doing. So far, 13 of 26 prostitutes have had a positive G.C. smear. I still think this is a futile effort though."[61]

Another task for the team involved providing immunizations for the locals. This dovetailed with the MILPHAP mission to improve the health of Vietnamese civilians. Sheldon wrote:

> We are in the beginning stages of what I fear is a hepatitis[62] epidemic. Mac and I are busily looking for carriers and passing out Gamma globulin.[63] We are trying to inoculate a group of about 400 people, and believe me this is a job. I had my Gamma Globulin this a.m. and I can hardly sit down. [64]

Finally, practicing medicine in a third world nation during wartime also exposed Sheldon to medical problems not seen in the United States. About six months into his tour, on September 10, 1968, Sheldon was sent to check out a possible epidemic of smallpox in a little Vietnamese village, far from Vinh Long, that had been hit by the Viet Cong on September 9. He was brought there by helicopter and noticed an airfield close to the border of Laos. When he asked why the airfield was there, Sheldon was told that it was to protect our military presence in Laos. After his investigation, he concluded that they did not have smallpox in the area.

Another unusual and unique incident occurred on November 12, 1968, after half his tour was finished. While he was at the compound, Sheldon received a note from one of the nurses at the hospital that stated: "Dear Dr. Kushner, We receive a 13-year-old female who was injured rectum by water buffalo here at 16.00. . . . Will you please come?"[65] Sheldon rushed to the hospital to take care of the problem, even though he had finished work that day.

Month after month, in the daily grind of multiple surgeries, whatever he learned at the University of Alabama Medical School would be repeatedly tested in the field on the innocent Vietnamese civilians—the victims of the war. This repetition was a learning experience, but his workload affected his emotional state and shaped his thinking about the war. As Sheldon explained to his wife, "I have mixed emotions. I see people who have been shot up and burned by us. Some of them are innocent people. It's very upsetting."[66]

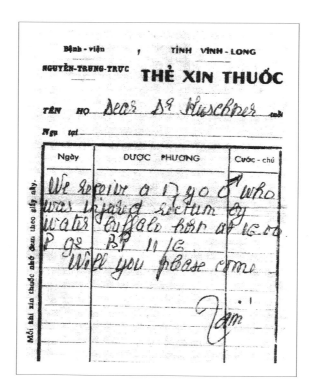

Note to Sheldon, asking for immediate help with a water buffalo injury

5

The Long Days of Surgery Make a Better Doctor

Today I had a very depressing day as I had the unpleasant job of doing 4 amputations.
On one little 7-year old boy, I had to do 2 above the knee amputations.
This gave me a very empty feeling and I almost cried. I know they had to be done,
but this little boy never did anything to anybody. What could a 7-year-old boy do?

Captain Sheldon Kushner, MD, July 1968

By his fourth month of service in Vinh Long, Sheldon had settled into a routine with his unit and used it as an opportunity to sharpen his skills as a surgeon. He summed up his long days of surgery in a letter to his wife:

> Every day here is about the same. I see an endless amount of blood, guts, gore and death. I have never seen so much death in my life. I saw more people die in two weeks than I saw during my entire medical school and internship period. The absolute butchery of human beings at times becomes overwhelming.[67]

The next day he added, "I wish there was something new to tell you about, but every day is the same; surgery, surgery, and more surgery,"[68] a sentiment repeated a few months later when he said, "I'm just working and sleeping and that's about it."[69] They performed surgery 12 hours a day, six and a half days a week, with a half day off on Sunday. He wrote, "I love those Sundays."[70]

Throughout this grueling schedule of four to six surgical procedures each day, one after another without rest, Sheldon wished he had more training:

> Every day, I just wish I knew more so I could provide more and better medical care to these people. I assure you, however, I will continue to do the absolute best I can. I just hope that this will be enough more often than not.[71]

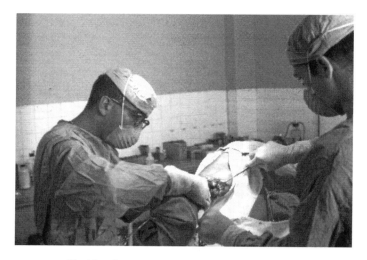

Sheldon in surgery, often 6-8 times each day

Looking back years later, Sheldon concluded, "I burned out on trauma surgery and went into obstetrics and gynecology when I returned from Vietnam."[72]

Part of Sheldon's routine included follow-up visits with patients to check on their progress. Examining, diagnosing and monitoring patients was part of their treatment. These bedside skills had been part of his medical school education and proved very useful in Vinh Long where the doctors had to build trust.

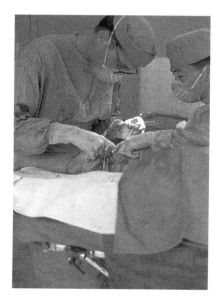

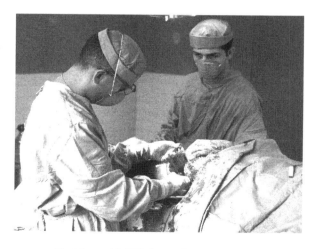

Sheldon with Bill Gates during surgery

Dr. McComb (Mac) with Ong Duong during surgery

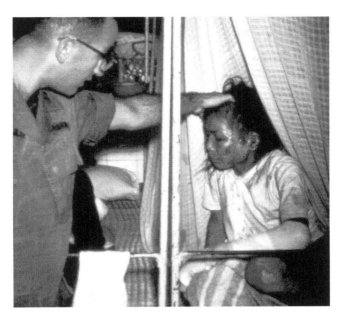

Typical day at the hospital would find Sheldon examining a patient

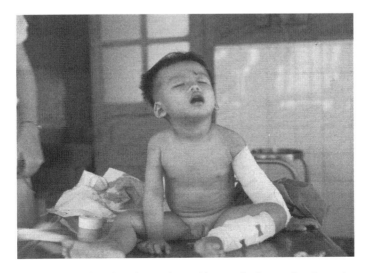

A child visibly showing pain and in need of more treatment

Downtime came each day after the pressure of surgery. The staff would enjoy beer and hors d'oeuvres at the hospital. Sheldon noted that the Vietnamese colleagues would try to see who could drink their beer the fastest. In particular, Mr. Nam and Mr. Yong, two Vietnamese medical technicians, raced to see who could outdo the others.

There are numerous examples of his workload in the letters and tapes Sheldon sent home to Carol. What can't be communicated are the sounds of pain and smells of vomiting, sweat, and blood in the hospital or operating room. In short, surgery was never dull and always at fever pitch, with an effort to ensure that each patient was cared for with the best the doctors could offer. Sheldon wrote about this on many occasions: "I'm sure I have done 10–12 major cases in the last 3 days. It's been a long time since I have been this tired."[73]

Surgical Downtime in Vinh Long

Mr. Nam challenging Sheldon in a glass-to-glass beer duel

Each of the men raises a glass during the beer challenge

Nurse Cathy shown on the left
with other members of the medical team

Tom Graue and the other team
members after surgery

Dr. Fred Seaman with the medics at a favorite restaurant, Long Chau's

He added a couple days later, "The civilian casualties are still pouring in so fast that it is absolutely unreal. The amount of surgery is just absolutely overwhelming."[74]

More cases than time became the norm for these doctors: "We are still busy as hell at the hospital and the surgery schedule every day is almost unbelievable. I am doing 4–5 cases each day and I would do more but time just doesn't allow it."[75]

Sometimes Sheldon's varied surgical experiences translated into his wondering what his future would be like after returning home from Vietnam. In April, Sheldon described himself this way: "Today I became an orthopedic surgeon. For the first time in my life I opened up a knee joint and got a bullet out of it. Messy as hell, but I got the job done, I think."[76] The next month he contemplated another direction: "Today was unreal in surgery. I found myself wiring a jaw together of all things. Hell, I might be an oral surgeon one day."[77] Months later, a third type of doctor was on his plate: "Tomorrow is a big day for me as I become a neurosurgeon. We are starting to do a little intracranial work."[78]

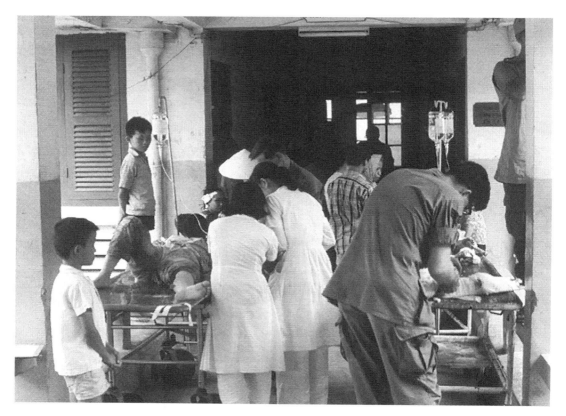

Doctors and nurses working on cases that had just arrived

His surgical experience in Vietnam had another effect: the terrific day-to-day workload eliminated the "Brownian movement" experienced by many doctors during surgery. When a surgeon lacks confidence, he or she can be seen bouncing around the operating room under the pressure and nerve-racking conditions—very much like the erratic, random movement of particles in a fluid that results from the continuous bombardment from molecules in the surrounding medium. Sheldon smiled as he explained:

> Visualize molecules dashing around. Under stressful surgical situations, some doctors have been known to start uttering repeatedly: 'Oh, my God,' Oh, my God,' accompanied by repetitive and rapid hand movements during the outburst.

Sheldon learned the importance of calmness under pressure and it became the norm because of Vietnam. As he explained,

> I learned that without the proper training, the proper equipment and without the proper support staff, a doctor must be creative and ultimately learn how to 'just stay with it.'[79]

When he returned to the States and worked, alongside other doctors in the operating room, Sheldon realized just how calm he was in these pressure situations.

For his surgical success and can-do attitude in Vietnam, Sheldon gives much credit to his former teacher, Dr. Holt McDowell:

> Because of him, there was nothing that I saw in Vinh Long that intimidated me. I saw a lot of stuff that I didn't know how to do, but I wasn't scared to learn how to do it and to try because I had the basics from Dr. McDowell. He instilled in me a keen sense of responsibility and I learned how essential that is in the care of patients.[80]

The severity of war wounds had become a typical part of the surgery experience and it was Sheldon's job, along with the whole medical team, to do whatever was necessary to deal with the cruelties of war:

> Last night I had to go to the hospital (with MP protection) to do a C-section on a 20 y.o. [year-old] girl 8 months pregnant who had been shot in the abdomen. The bullet went right through the neck and head of the fetus. So after a quiet day I had an exciting night. When I finished that case last night I had to do a laparotomy[81] on a teenage boy.[82]

At times, Sheldon was very frustrated because he wasn't formally trained to do all these surgeries and often patients died. "I know we did a lot of good things but you remember the ones that didn't work. It's hard not to blame yourself," he noted.[83] One case that haunts him to this day is the double leg amputation he performed on a small seven-year-old boy named Loc.

Loc's mother had carried him into the hospital. He had stepped on something that tore open both of his legs. They were badly mangled, and there was evidence of gas gangrene probably from clostridium perfringens bacteria.[84] "He was clinically septic and I knew that he would die if we did not act quickly," said Sheldon.[85] With surgery and antibiotics, Loc survived, but Sheldon had to perform a few additional surgical procedures on Loc's stumps.

Later he sent a picture of Loc to his wife and wrote on the back of it:

> This is Loc, and I will confess that it broke my heart to have to cut both of his legs off. He is 7 years old and he happened to get in the way. What difference does it make whose mortars hit him? Loc represents part of the tragedy that is Vietnam. We all fell in love with this one.[86]

Sheldon became attached to Loc; he taught Loc some English and read to him when he had time. Sheldon brought his tape recorder to the hospital and recorded a conversation with Loc. Sheldon later sent the tape to his wife.

Sheldon's mother sent toys for Loc, and the Navy Seabees built him a wheelchair.

A closeup of Loc with crutches

Sheldon's handwritten notes to home about Loc

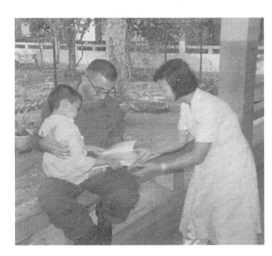

Loc, shown here with Sheldon, his nurse and
the books that came from Sheldon's mother,
Rose Kushner

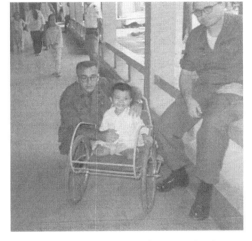

The wheelchair built by the Navy Seabees
especially for Loc

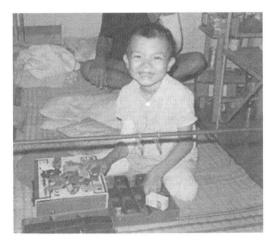

Loc playing with toys after surgery
that were a gift from Sheldon's mother

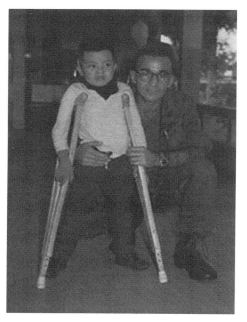

Sheldon and Loc

Loc getting used to his new legs with a
little help from Sheldon

Another photo of Loc with his new legs supported by his crutches and Sheldon

"We were able to obtain artificial legs for Loc, and, with the help of crutches, he was able to walk. After he was released, Loc's mother brought him to the hospital to see me from time to time," he explained.[87] Sheldon gave Loc storybooks, coloring books, and other children's books, all in English. He promised Loc that if he read them, he would be given more books.

Several months after Sheldon returned to the United States in 1969, he received a letter from a Vietnamese nurse who had worked with him in the hospital. She said that Loc came to see Sheldon and cried when he was told that Dr. Kushner was not there. Loc's mother turned him over to his grandmother to provide his care. Then the grandmother sent him to live in a rehab hospital in Saigon, and he was not happy there. Sheldon lost contact with his nurse and has never heard from anyone in Vinh Long since that time. This case haunts him to this day. It was heartbreaking to amputate the legs of a child, especially given the difficulty of being a double amputee in a country with little medical treatment available.

Sheldon's surgical experiences in Vietnam made him a better doctor upon returning to the States, but it took a lot out of him. While Sheldon honed his skills, there were many challenges that affected his mind, body, and emotional state.

6

Medical Challenges
Bring Creative Medicine

Today was another one of those dreadful days and again I spent almost the entire day in the operating room. This morning I went down to make rounds as I usually do on Sunday. However, instead of leaving right after rounds, I found myself there, operating until 2:00 p.m.

Captain Sheldon Kushner, MD, September 1968

Sheldon quickly learned that the wartime circumstances in Vinh Long had an impact on the range of surgeries he performed in the hospital. Practicing medicine in Vinh Long meant treating injuries rarely or never seen during his days in Alabama. But other challenges surfaced as well.

Dysentery was a problem for Vietnamese patients and even the doctors, and Sheldon saw much cirrhosis of the liver in the injured Vietnamese. People who lived on the Mekong River used the water for both cooking and bathing. Although cirrhosis was associated with alcohol use, in most cases it was a result of scaring that occurred because of contracting hepatitis from the unsanitary conditions.

The homes or hooches along the Mekong were both a home, a wash basin and the source of drinking water for the inhabitants. As a result, when Sheldon and his team opened a wound, they would often find parasites. In many cases, they even found nematode worms (Ascaris[88]) in the intestines.[89]

Most of the civilian injuries were from guns—M-16s (whose bullets traveled at 3,200 feet per second) or AK-47s (whose bullets traveled at 2,000 feet per second)—or from missiles.

In addition to treating the Vietnamese and many GIs for venereal disease, Sheldon treated one patient for tetanus,[90] which was the first case he ever treated as a young doctor.[91]

Sheldon saw many types of injuries while working in the hospital. The wounds were endemic of people's living along the waterways or in a town surrounded by rural countryside and dirt roads. A patient might arrive with a crushed leg, a head wound from a truck tire or with infant growth issues.

Hooches (also spelled Hootch, is a simple hut or dwelling) along
canal for both washing and obtaining drinking water

Flight surgeon Capt. Gerald McGowan, in "Military Medicine to Win Hearts and Minds,"wrote that he would see eight to ten burn patients a day, many resulting "from using purloined [pilfered, looted, or appropriated] jet fuel as household fuel."[92]

The MILPHAP team would need to work quickly to save lives. Many included amputations that required cleaning and closure, explained in detail further in this chapter as "delayed primary closure."

Sheldon would use his own Craig 212 tape recorder to listen to tapes from a resident he knew from medical school, Bob Yoder. These tapes contained instructions, based on questions Sheldon had asked, on how to perform several types of surgeries. Sheldon would use these tapes, along with medical books his wife sent to him, to do unfamiliar surgeries. In a letter to his wife he wrote, "I'm sure that Grant's Atlas of Anatomy and the OB-GYN Journal will be coming along soon. We all need them, and I am pretty sure I have them at home. Grant's is a really big book."[93]

Doctors from his medical school days also provided instruction. Dr. Dan Merck sent him information about surgical procedures. Dr. Bill Harris sent a letter to him with hints about surgery. Sheldon also corresponded with Dr. Holt McDowell, the vascular surgeon with whom he had trained for three months during medical school. He, too, sent Sheldon audiotapes to assist him with unfamiliar surgeries.

Civilians Need Immediate Treatment

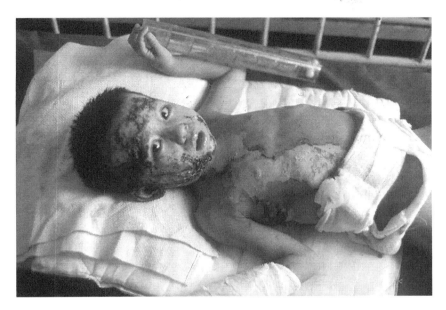

This child was brought into the hospital with gasoline burns;
shown is the healing after the third week of treatment

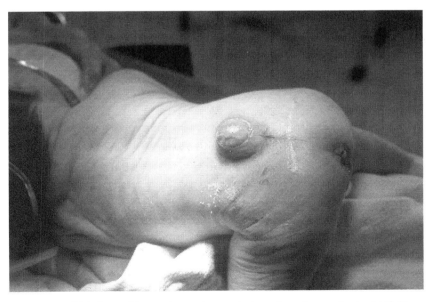

A 3-day old infant with myelomeningocele (a serious form of spinal bifida,
where the spinal cord and the spinal canal do not form or close normally)

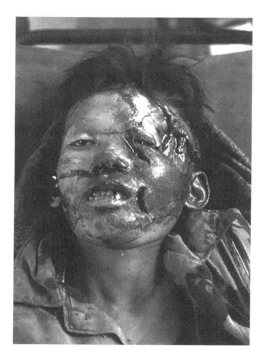

Teen run over by a truck

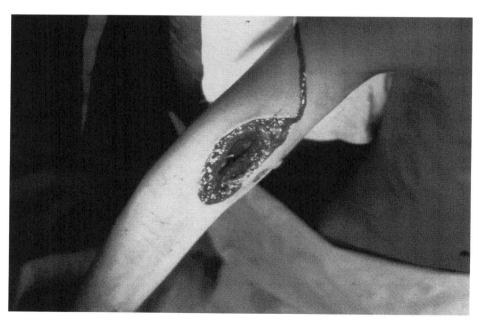

Bullet wound in the arm before surgury.
Wound size can determine what weapon was used

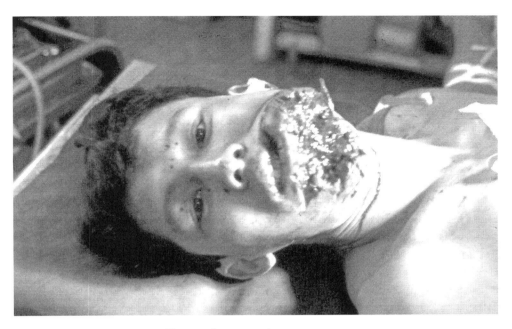

Trauma face wound pre-op surgery

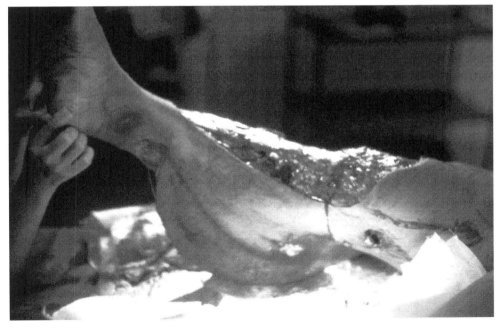

A 37-year old male with leg crushed between two barges
had to receive immediate care to save his life

At times Sheldon could get a ride to Saigon to obtain supplies and to speak with other doctors to get medical advice. In October of 1968 Sheldon traveled to Tokyo for a few days via Clark Air Force Base in the Philippines. There were three flights out of this base using C-141 medical planes. One would fly into Cameron Bay, one would fly into Danang, and one would fly into Saigon. They would take planeloads of wounded soldiers to Tatchakawa Air Force base near Tokyo, which had better facilities for their care. Sheldon consulted with many physicians there so he would be better equipped to service his patients in Vinh Long.

At the same time that Sheldon and his team were receiving outside help, they weren't being fully supported by the existing Vietnamese medical staff at Vinh Long. He was frequently told by American military and civilian workers that the South Vietnamese government and army, who ran the hospital at night, were corrupt and were taking the antibiotics and selling them to the Viet Cong.[94]

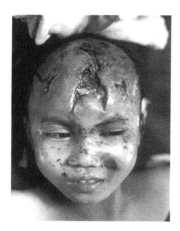 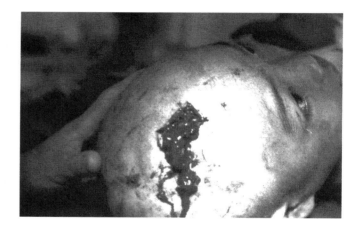

A 12-year old female (left) and another patient shown here with frag wounds from a rocket, luckily without any skull penetration

Because of the enormous workload of about 200 surgeries a month per doctor, Sheldon and his medical colleagues devised strategies and protocols that they would follow based upon their abilities, equipment, and supplies. In this way, they used the resources that were available to help the greatest number of patients survive. For example, Sheldon and Mac chose not to do thoracotomies (opening the chest) because they did not have the equipment to do this surgery or care for a post-operative thoracotomy patient. Such surgery was extremely dangerous for the patient when the doctors did not have respirators or chest suction devices at their disposal, and when they lacked the support staff to care for these patients. Therefore, Sheldon and Mac devised a protocol to treat chest injuries with more conservative techniques, resulting in varying degrees of success and failure.

Ether was the only general anesthesia available, and it was generally safe—except that any nearby electric current could cause an explosion if it came in contact with the ether. "We had Vietnamese nurse anesthetists who were good with administering anesthesia using only ether," he said. They would take moist towels and wrap them around the hosing to guard against the ether exploding. Unfortunately, they had no muscle relaxants to use with the anesthesia, which made the surgery more difficult than it already was, because they had to fight stiff muscles while operating. The doctors also administered spinal and axillary block anesthetics when necessary.[95]

The medical team did not have a blood bank and were sometimes able to obtain blood from a relative, but the team soon discovered that the Vietnamese population felt uncomfortable about blood transfusions, an unfamiliar procedure in their culture. When blood could be obtained, the team had no means of type and cross matching the blood, so they had to improvise. They discovered that if the donor blood did not clump when mixed with patient blood, that donor blood was generally safe to use. As Sheldon said, "When the patient has a low blood count and is exsanguinating [bleeding out], there is nothing to lose by trying the available blood. We didn't have a wide range of volume expanding products available in Vinh Long." They also had no access to blood substitutes.[96]

Trauma Surgery

Pre-op hand trauma surgery

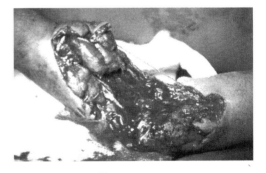

Pre-op elbow trauma surgery

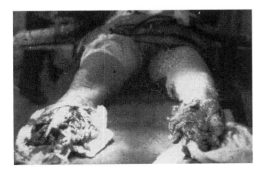

Pre-op leg amputation trauma surgery

Pre-op foot surgery on a jerry-rigged stirrup

Similarly, Tom Graue, the medic who worked with Sheldon, remarked how the Vietnamese culture had a visible effect on the medical treatment: "The Vietnamese had marks on their temples of their head and on the bridges of their noses. They used Chinese medicine to squeeze the area for blood to get rid of their headaches. They also used suction cups."[97]

Head injuries posed difficult challenges for these doctors. During a visit to the Tan Son Nhut Air Force Base Officer's Club near Saigon, Sheldon met a neurosurgeon who taught him how to do a craniotomy[98] for those patients. The neurosurgical procedure required part of the skull to be removed in order to take out tissue and provide room for the swelling brain, as well as to control bleeding.

Sheldon shared the knowledge and techniques with Mac after returning to Vinh Long. Thereafter, Sheldon and Mac started doing these procedures with a great degree of success.

Pre-op hygiene was the norm for the MILPHAP team

Tom Graue recalled how he helped Sheldon during surgery: "On one occasion, we had to remove a bullet from a woman's brain and while I read the textbook, telling him how to do it, the operation went well. The woman lived and did not have disabilities when she left their care."[99]

Vascular injuries were common in Vietnam. To create protocols for such injuries, Sheldon communicated with various surgical physicians in Birmingham, Alabama, who instructed him on how to repair damaged arteries and how to use venous (vein) grafts when necessary. Sheldon also recalled his vascular surgery experience under Dr. McDowell:

> I learned a lot watching Dr. McDowell operate and that was a big help to me in Vietnam. . . . It was always amazing to me that these vascular repairs and grafts usually worked, and that was without the benefit of anticoagulants like Heparin[100] or without low molecular weight Dextran[101] to enhance the blood flow,[102] or (Reo) Macrodex[103] to keep blood from clotting.

Without background knowledge of veins, they used an anatomy atlas opened to the correct pages to find what they were looking for.

When a vascular injury did occur, it needed immediate repair because blood vessels serviced other parts of the body. Vein grafting was the answer. Dr. Bob Yoder reminded Sheldon that in grafting a vein, the valves have to be in the right direction. Stitching was done using fine silk. In addition, despite not having these medicines, surgery usually turned out well.[104]

Delayed Primary Closure

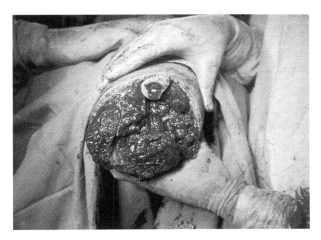

Grenade trap wound before surgery. Shown is the wound amputed, cleaned and debrided

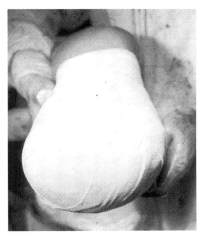

The wound is covered for a period of time and rechecked often to determine whether any infection has set in

Closure of the wound (above): After being reexamined and if it looks clean, the wound is in the process of being closed, with the last step (right) being the delayed primary closure

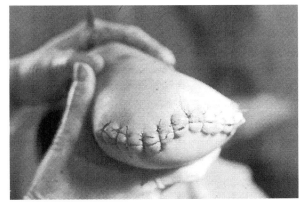

A wound that is sealed like this is carefully monitored by the doctors

In the environment of a hospital that did not have the medical amenities often found in American hospitals in 1968, the surgical principles of "debridement"[105] and "delayed primary closure"[106] were very important to Sheldon in Vietnam. He explained,

All the war injuries to these civilians in Vietnam had to be considered to be dirty with bacteria and in fact, most of them were visibly dirty. High velocity missile injuries from AK-47 and M-16 weapons, as well as from Claymore mines, all had tissue damage that could not always be recognized immediately.[107]

In one instance, an 18-year old male arrived with a severe leg wound from a grenade trap that required BK (below the knee) amputation. These traps could be set anywhere along walking paths and made impossible to see. For the doctors, they employed every tool in their surgeon's bag of tricks from their study and experiences to save lives. One method shown here is described by Sheldon as "delayed primary closure."

A Claymore mine had a trip wire and used nails as projectiles; injuries from these mines required the surgeon to assess tissue damage as there was a small entry wound and a large exit wound. The procedure for these dirty wounds was to use surgical debridement until they were clean and all nonviable tissue had been removed. In other words, the proper procedure would be to clean up the wound or debride it, and then later either close the wound or clean it out more.

It often took about a week to 10 days until the wound could be closed. Even when the doctors amputated part of the body, they did not close the stub immediately. Sheldon noted, "After this had been accomplished, delayed primary closure of the wounds was performed. An understanding of this surgical principle was a great help to me for the rest of my medical career." Over time, Sheldon could actually tell if an injury had been caused by an AK-47 or a M-16 since he had seen so many of them.[108]

Napalm burns were very common in Vietnam, and yet they were extremely difficult to treat under the conditions there. Caring for these burns requires highly skilled nursing care and a sterile environment, neither of which were available in Vinh Long. High-percentage burns (those that cover 40–50 percent of the body) are associated with tremendous systemic problems—dehydration, infection, and malnutrition. Because the doctors did not have a sterile environment or the nursing care or the type of nutritional support required for high-percentage burns, the patients did not do well. In treating these injuries, Sheldon relied on his University Hospital experience in Birmingham, Alabama, where he treated burn victims.

In Vinh Long, he spent many hours performing split thickness skin grafts using a Brown dermatome, an instrument for cutting thin skin slices for grafting. When the patients were stabilized and the burn eschars (scabs) had been debrided over time, the burn areas were covered with split thickness skin grafts usually obtained from the inside of the thigh.

When the donor sites healed, the doctors repeatedly went back to those areas to harvest more skin.

Mac (Dr. Gordon McComb) was responsible for the care of a ten-year old female patient with painful napalm burns requiring multiple surgeries. She had severely burned lower extremities and her toes were destroyed. Mac grafted her many times until she was completely covered. She survived but walked with difficulty.

Sheldon and his team also performed orthopedic surgery. This, too, was on-the-job training. Although Sheldon had no training or experience doing cast work, he observed it on his orthopedic rotation as a medical student. After finishing his internship in June 1967 and before entering the Air Force in September 1967, he worked in the Thuss Clinic, an industrial medical clinic, where he also saw cast work, but again had no hands-on experience with it.

However, the corpsmen he worked with were very skilled in casting. He recalled how one corpsman, Sergeant Bill Grover, a medic for many years, had shown him how to put Kirschner, or K, wires in a femur. Although the equipment Sheldon had to insert these wires was obsolete in U.S. hospitals at this time, it was all he had to use in Vinh Long. Bill was familiar with this equipment and taught Sheldon how to use it. With Bill's assistance, Sheldon's medical learning curve decreased. "My corpsmen were invaluable," he remarked.[109]

Napalm's Effects on Patient

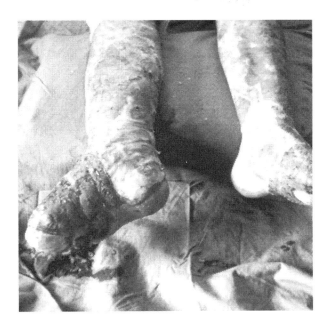

The 10-year old could stand with difficulty and a closeup of her wounds
reveals the task that lay ahead for Mac

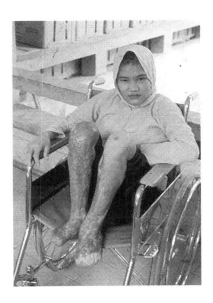

Post-op in a wheelchair and going home to her family

The Art of Skin Grafting

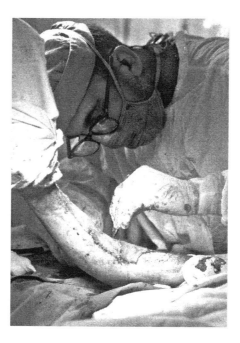

Sheldon performing a skin graft

Gathering the skin

The brown dermatome during the grafting

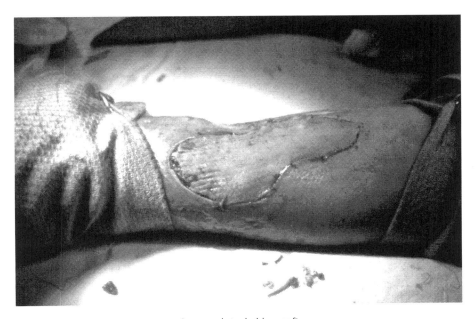

A completed skin graft

Corpsman Bill Grover was also a master at getting things; he once told Sheldon, "Doc, while you are over here, if there's anything you need, just tell me; I'll get it for you." Sheldon replied, "What are you talking about? Supplies?" Bill answered, "I said 'anything you need.' But there's two rules: never ask me where I got it and never ask me to take it back."[110]

Grover was as good as his word. Sheldon explained,

> We were driving back to our quarters at 8:00 at night. We weren't looking forward to the garbage we were fed from that [compound] kitchen. I told Grover I'd like to have a nice T-bone steak. He said, "Maybe one of these days." A few nights later, I went up to my room and there were boxes everywhere—200 T-bone steaks. I said to Grover, "What the hell is this?" He said, "These are the T-bone steaks you wanted." I said, "We don't need 200 of them." Grover said, "I can't take them back." So we had a party. [111]

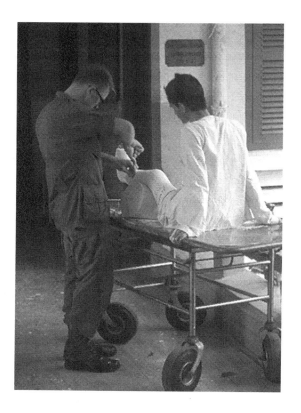

One of several Corpsman, Titus Herr, is shown here completing a full leg "casting"

The gift that keeps on giving continued with Grover. Sheldon and his team had three jeeps that never worked, so they had to push them every day to get them started. He recounted,

> When we were coming back from work one night, I said to Grover, This is a pain in the ass. I wish we had a jeep we didn't have to push off all of the time. A few weeks later, I noticed parked in my parking spot at the compound, a jeep with freshly painted decals on it. I said, What the hell? Grover replied, You wanted another jeep? Sheldon noted, I think he stole it from a general at the army airfield nearby.[112]

"If it were not for Grover, a lot of people would have died. He would get supplies in a hurry for us,"[113] Sheldon concluded. Indeed, their unit was not a high priority. Their supply of antibiotics was limited to penicillin and Chloromycetin, which were two standard antibiotics adequate for treating the infections Sheldon and his team saw during surgery. Sheldon called this a major medical management problem and a major infection problem. "Oddly enough, they did have an abundance of 50 percent dextrose, which was useless unless you had many diabetic patients," said Sheldon.[114]

Another medical challenge the doctors faced came when they had to fulfill the MILPHAP mission: to train the Vietnamese doctors at the hospitals. There was only one, Bacsi Gian, serving with Sheldon, Mac, and Fred at Vinh Long, and throughout his tour, Sheldon often voiced the frustrations that existed between him and his Vietnamese counterpart, beginning less than a month into his service, when he told his wife in an audiotape,

> He wants us to help him and do it his way. He won't listen to American advice. It's really frustrating. Look at the money we are putting into the hospital and the money we are putting into these villages and all the civic action programs around here to rebuild that village and to buy tractors for these farmers. They just don't care. I don't know what we should do. It's a bad situation. Everyone is confused and frustrated. It's hard not to get emotionally involved. I just want to get the hell out of here. I was so hawkish in the States and I'm ready to get out of here and let the Vietnamese have Vietnam.[115]

Sheldon again expressed his thoughts in August of 1968 in an audiotape to his wife:

> The Vietnamese doctor that worked with us in the hospital thinks he knows it all and wants to do everything his way. I know that what's wrong is wrong. . . . He would often write orders for drugs not indicated by me. He would be stealing my patients because I tried to keep them separate from his. He couldn't save some, but he wouldn't let the American doctors help his patients, even though we could do better. His hospital training seemed inferior to ours. [116]

The only Vietnamese doctor counterpart, Basci Gian who was troubling
to the American doctors is sitting to the right of Sheldon and Fred

Less than a month later Sheldon wrote with more detail:

> Guess what? This new colonel here, who is really a No. 1 man, has put the
> cards on the table. He told us that if we are not satisfied with our counterpart,
> he will help us get rid of him. If we could get a Vietnamese physician or
> physicians here who could learn to take care of these people properly, then
> maybe we could prevent one American doctor somewhere from having to
> come over here or even maybe more. The purpose of our mission here in this
> hospital and in Vietnam in general, is to eliminate the need for our presence
> here. When we can do this, no more Americans will have to make the same
> sacrifice that you and I are making and even more importantly, no more
> Americans will have to make that awful sacrifice that has already been made
> by over 26,000 Americans. I really don't know if we can ever eliminate the
> need for our presence here.[117]

Days before President Johnson announced a total halt to U.S. bombing in North
Vietnam, Sheldon and his colleagues finally confronted their medical counterpart. In a letter
to Carol, dated October 28, 1968, Sheldon reported that on that day, he and his colleagues
finally sat down with Bacsi Gian.[118] They explained that many things he was doing were
below acceptable American medical standards, but he had no interest in their opinions and
was resistant to change. His reaction could be attributed to the fact that Vietnamese are very
proud people, and taking the advice of American doctors could be viewed as losing face.
Sheldon recalls, "He and I parted on a friendly note, but I think he was probably happy
when I finished my tour in Vinh Long."[119]

By January 1969, Sheldon's tour was nearing its end. He began to transfer his workload to his counterpart. He wrote, "I am trying to cut back on the amount of surgery that I will be doing and am trying to increase the load of my counterpart even more."[120]

Sheldon could cheer about something that shows his personal disdain for the counterpart when he declared, victoriously:

> Well . . . today I celebrated my birthday by having a real knock down drag out argument with my counterpart. Honey, I am a real "hot head" and I know it and I am not proud of it, but sometimes I just can't help it. However, I do have one attribute that I am proud of and that being that I am not afraid to stand up for what I think is right. I have always been a man of high principle, at least I have tried to be, and when the day comes that I start compromising my principles, I will essentially be nothing.[121]

These challenges helped Sheldon become an experienced surgeon. Working with a team, day in and day out, and dealing with multiple personalities and the varieties of surgeries unlike anything seen in Alabama, prepared him, like nothing else could, for any situation in which he would find himself when he returned to the States. At the same time, the experiences in Vinh Long took a physical and psychological toll on the young surgeon.

7

Physical and Psychological Impact

The war is raging at a fantastic pace now and Honey, it is vicious. I see the results of it every day

and we are still working ourselves into exhaustion. Believe me, even the emergency room

[in Birmingham, Alabama] never even approached this.

Captain Sheldon Kushner, MD, June 10, 1968

In addition to coping with his work environment in the hospital, Sheldon experienced physical and psychological effects from his service in Vinh Long. As he told his wife, "The food was awful and the stress was unbelievable—the work load was unreal." After just two months, Sheldon lost 20 pounds.[122] It was not a pleasant existence. He repeatedly wrote about his exhaustion. Typical was what he wrote to Carol on May 23, 1968: "I came in last night at 8:00 p.m. so completely exhausted that I ate supper and then just collapsed on the bed."[123]

Although they had a kitchen with a chef at the compound, they could not always get food since their facility was not a high priority on the supply chain for food. At times items had to be airlifted to them. Sheldon remembers having a can of sea rations (cold ham and lima beans) that was not very appealing at six in the morning when it was 110 degrees outside. However, Sheldon's father sent many cans of food from the family grocery store to supplement his son's diet.

Less than a month into his tour of duty, Sheldon got sick from the food. He wrote:

> Today has been the worst day I have experienced here. The food here, even though purchased in the U.S., can really make you sick as hell and today I got it [diarrhea]. However, I am feeling better now and by the time you get this letter I am sure I will be a well man. Everybody here gets it regularly and it is just something you must learn to tolerate.[124]

Sheldon and the other doctors were frequently sick. They were constantly getting colds and fevers and other ailments that were more of an annoyance than any hindrance to being on duty. He once told Carol, "Right now I am taking steroids and antihistamines to combat an urticarial rash." [125] An urticarial rash is an allergic response to anything—insects, food, foliage, medications, or something else. There is no way to tell where Sheldon's came from in Vietnam.[126] In another letter from November 3, 1968, Sheldon noted, "Believe it or not, I have been sick again since Saturday night. This time I have the intestinal flu."[127] In a letter dated January 3, 1969, Sheldon again indicated that he and Mac were sick.

In addition to sickness, Sheldon often expressed fear in his letters about what was happening in Vinh Long. Like most other servicemen, he described his time in country as a scary and horrifying experience. He still has nightmares from his tour of duty and suffers from PTSD.

It was usually difficult for him to sleep at night once he left the hospital. There was no air conditioning in the compound, although Sheldon did have a fan in his room. Mortars and rockets and sniper fire often disrupted his sleep. At times, he and other members of the compound had to vacate the premises because of an attack.

Less than a month after his arrival in Vietnam, Sheldon told his wife in an audiotape, "The NRVN [South Vietnamese] troops are an ungrateful lazy group of people not interested in winning the war. These people don't want to fight at night." [128]

Sheldon became increasingly sensitive to the frequent raids and bombings; the tension began to permeate much of the writing to his wife:

> We are busy as hell here. I can't get caught up with all the surgery I have to do. . . . Last night we got quite a bit of mortar fire, but no harm done to us. The town, however, got zapped, thus I end up in surgery all day. Do you remember that loud thunder we heard? Well, multiply that by 10, and that is how loud these mortars sound when they come in. [129]

Bombs before loading onto a B-52

Similarly, he wrote on May 17th, "This morning I was awakened by a noise like I have never heard before. The whole house was shaking and I thought the world was coming to an end. The noise was a B-52 strike about 15 miles away."[130]

While peace talks were scheduled to begin on May 10, 1968, by May 5, Sheldon reported enemy activity:

> There has been a definite increase in V.C. activities in this area. However, the V.C. in this area fight a guerilla war here consisting mainly of snipers, ambushes, and mortars. The mortars are the only things I have to worry about. This province, like most provinces in Vietnam is entirely owned by Charlie at night, except for the town of Vinh Long. During the day, Charlie owns about half the province. There are already about 1,500 American military personnel here. However, today we received 1,000 new men, which is two air cavalry battalions. With them came 80 new helicopters. So the defense of the area is really building up.[131]

Bombing run from B-52's

The source of the noise heard from miles away by Sheldon during a night time bombing raid; this explosion lit up the night sky

Bombs find their targets

When an offensive by the Viet Cong was about to begin, Sheldon would mentally prepare by writing to his wife:

> As you have probably read in the papers, the V.C. have started another nationwide offensive, certainly trying to gain bargaining power for the Paris peace talks which begin in 4 days. Here we received about 30–40 mortar rounds on the airfield Saturday night, all was quiet last night. Tonight everyone is ready and alert.[132]

Huey Cobra Helicopters or Snake, is a Bell AH-1 Cobra two-blade copter

Several days later, on May 12, 1968, he reported to his wife: "This morning some of our rangers demolished a couple of hundred V.C. who were lurking about the airfield. They described it as a good kill. War is awful, isn't it?"[133] And the next day he reflected on the cost of killing a single sniper by saying:

> A V.C. sniper just opened fire on our house and he received in return about 250 rounds of M-16 fire. They brought him in to me and he actually looked like a big piece of hamburger meat. 250 rounds to kill 1 V.C.! The Army estimates that it costs about $250,000 to kill one V.C. For 1/250 of that we could probably talk the same guy into coming over to our side.[134]

Casualties mounted, and on May 16th Sheldon concluded, "The civilian casualties are still pouring in and I can't remember when I was as tired as I am now. I am 100% exhausted. I have never seen so many badly injured people at one time."[135]

Huey gunship Bell UH-1 Iroquois (nicknamed "Huey") is a
utility military helicopter with a 40 mm grenade launcher.

Huey gunships returning from a mission

B-52 Airstrikes

Sheldon's letters communicated the intensity of the war from his vantage point in Vinh Long. He wrote, "The war is raging at a fantastic pace now and Honey, it is vicious. I see the results of it every day and we are still working ourselves into exhaustion. Believe me, even the emergency room [in Birmingham, Alabama] never even approached this."[136] In an audiotape he made on June 16, 1968, he told Carol, "The airfield gets mortared every night and the base gets it too."[137] A letter he wrote on June 23, 1968, emphasized the increasing pace of the war in more detail: "The war is raging at an alarming rate. Some of our people are right now in heavy contact with a V.C. Battalion in Vinh Binh, a subsection of Vinh Long Province. I can feel the air strikes 40 miles away. Tomorrow will be a busy day for me."[138]

By July, the military situation hadn't changed much: "After a few days of relative quiet, things perked up a bit last night as the town got hit pretty hard with mortars. Actually I slept through all of that but I did find a hospital full of wounded patients this a.m."[139] He repeated to his wife two days later: "The casualties are coming in again. I bet that I have already done 250–300 major cases since I have been here, and it doesn't look like things are going to change."[140] The whole experience was affecting his psychological state, and he shared that feeling with Carol: "I have overcome my depression for the time being and hope you are feeling better. I guess that's what a tour in Vietnam is: a series of depressions until one happy day when all of a sudden it is all over."[141]

On July 24, he told his wife, "The tension is growing and growing in expectation of that new offensive. . . . When and if this offensive comes, it certainly won't be a surprise to anyone."[142] On July 31, 1968, things began to heat up. Sheldon wrote, "Last night the V.C. really drove the rockets and mortars into the airfield. Fortunately, no one was hurt. I climbed down from the ceiling at about 3:00 a.m. and went back to sleep. Those damn things are loud as hell."[143] Later, in an audiotape, Sheldon did recall that "two civilian engineers were killed."[144]

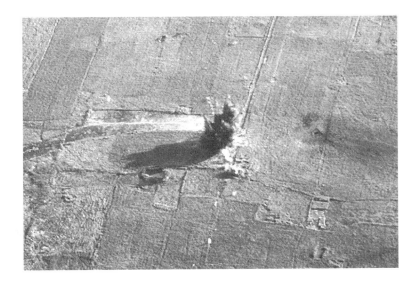

B-52 airstrike finds its target

Through his letters, by August of 1968, Sheldon indicated that there was another offensive. His personal safety was always on his mind, but he told his wife, "I take great comfort in the fact that we have over twice as many Americans in this area as they had during TET."[145] On August 22, 1968, he noted, "As you are probably reading in the paper we are getting plenty of action in this area. The civilian casualties are more numerous now than I have seen since I have been here."[146] The letters continued as the strikes came more often. On August 27, he wrote about one particular attack:

> Last night the V.C. hit the airfield with the heaviest mortar and ground attack I have seen since I have been here. Actually, I sat by my window and watched every single bit of it, the V.C. mortars and the allied reactionary helicopter attacks. However, I am OK, so don't worry about me.[147]

The next day, he reported, "Last night the V.C. hit the town again with a mortar attack, but I slept through it all."[148]

By the end of September 1968, Sheldon aired his frustrations with the war in a tape recording to his wife. After six months living in a war zone, he commented on the progress of the war: "I am beginning to believe we will never win this war. The cause is so vague and indefinite I don't know what we are fighting for. It's very depressing."[149] In a letter dated September 13, 1968, he questioned the ability of the South Vietnamese to defend themselves:

> Today another American Army battalion moved into the Vinh Long area. The more, the merrier, as far as I'm concerned. However, I think it's becoming more evident the Vietnamese military cannot take care of this area without our help. This of course was the original plan, to let the Vietnamese take care of the Delta area themselves with Americans functioning only as advisors.[150]

By October, Sheldon's letters included more conclusions about what he saw and felt about the war. Sheldon summed up his thinking on the military situation, saying that there was a need for a peace settlement. He wrote,

> The war activity is markedly decreased. There are several speculations about why. Some people feel that the V.C. are really saving up for a big push, some feel that they are seriously waiting for a peace settlement, others feel that the V.C. have really been beaten down badly and that the war is approaching an end. We will see.[151]

On October 31, President Johnson called a halt to the bombing of North Vietnam and the next day, Sheldon commented, "I just received the news about the bombing halt. I certainly hope that this means that a real peace is not far away. I pray to God every night that this senseless war can come to an end some day."[152]

The Viet Cong had another idea in mind. On November 3, Sheldon reported, "The V.C. responded to our bombing halt by mortaring the hell out of Vinh Long City last night. I hope that the bombing halt doesn't backfire on us. It is now about 1:15 a.m. Monday morning and I can't sleep."[153] In subsequent letters he noted that there had been an increase in surgery in the hospital. He said that the South Vietnamese were unhappy with the bombing halt. He and the other GIs had mixed feelings about it. Later in the month, Sheldon wrote, "The Vietnamese Regional Forces, similar to our National Guard, just received a big shipment of M-16 rifles and I believe they are just shooting up the countryside."[154]

During December, Sheldon and his colleagues were still busy with a heavy schedule of surgeries. He mentioned that he had 90 more days "in country" and commented, "I even love to talk about leaving this dreadful place."[155] At the end of the month he wrote about more Viet Cong activity:

> Today I was busy at the hospital. A V.C. terror squad placed a bomb in a school classroom and it really messed a few people up pretty badly. However, I think I have learned to relax a little more now. I just do the most I can, the best I can, and I don't seem to worry about all this quite as much. It is still so depressing and so far removed from reality as we know it.[156]

He also looked ahead to the situation in January 1969 when he wrote, "Everyone is looking toward next month, with caution, as the Tet Lunar New Year will be coming soon. When that is over, I know that everyone will be quite relieved."[157]

They, of course, were thinking about the previous year's Tet Offensive and hoping it wouldn't be repeated. On January 2, 1969, Sheldon reported an incident of friendly fire:

> Today was a really big one for us here in Vinh Long. One of the helicopter pilots accidently fired a bunch of rockets right into the middle of town. People were killed immediately. 2 more died at the hospital and 2 more probably will die. I took 2 of them to surgery and Mac took 2. We ended up the day today doing 6 major cases each. I certainly hope that this is noindication as to what the coming year will be like. [158]

Later in the month he again expressed his ongoing fear for his personal safety when he wrote his wife: "You don't have to apologize for being scared. I am scared too and I have been since I have been over here. Yes, everyone is quite tense in anticipation of a Tet Offensive."[159] He reiterated this feeling about the Tet Lunar New Year in letters he wrote on January 25 and on January 30. By February, he mentioned that his counterpart had a big Tet Party at the hospital. He wrote, "We are on 24 hour alert and no one is supposed to be out of the compound after 6:00 p.m. The team got permission to go anyway, but I declined."[160]

By this time his tour was almost completed and he did not want to take any chances. On February 17, the first day of Tet, Sheldon remarked, "I have been telling everyone that I am too short to get into a long conversation. Being short is fun, but it's also scary." So when one of the army officers stationed in a small outpost just outside of town about 15 miles, asked him and Mac to ride out with him to see the outpost, he declined. He told his wife: "This isn't a very healthy country to go sightseeing."[161]

On February 23, the Viet Cong attacked 110 targets throughout South Vietnam, including Saigon. Sheldon mentioned this offensive in a letter from that day:

> I will leave Vinh Long two weeks from today. The very thought of leaving Vinh Long just makes me feel good all over. I just hope that things are quiet in the Saigon area so I don't have any difficulty getting out of there. I still can't believe that this is for real, that this nightmare is really almost over with. I am sure that by now you have heard about the new nationwide offensive. Well, let me assure you that I am OK. So far all the fighting is out in the rural areas. It is still not known how big of an offensive this will turn out to be. I promise I am being ultra-careful.[162]

BART STARR

March 4, 1969

Dear Sheldon:

Some how words fail me when I try to express my feelings to thank you for your nice letter which arrived a few days ago.

Your thoughts are most appreciated and coming from someone like you possess even more meaning and impact. Before I began dictating this note, I mentioned how I had seen you and your family grow up merely across the street and believe me, it gives us alot of pleasure to know that you and your brothers have been willing to make the sacrifices and dedicated effort necessary to become the fine men you are today.

Cherry and I both hope this note finds you and your wife in great health and that you have a speedy return from Vietnam. Should you and Carol like to take a slight detour (!) in your return to Alabama, we would be delighted to show you some real Yankee hospitality.

Thanks again for your note and best wishes.

Sincerely,

Bart

Letter from Bart Starr, dated March 4, 1969

Sheldon's letters from the next two days indicated that although those two days were busy with surgery, he was still unsure of the magnitude of the offensive. He reiterated that activity was centered in the rural areas. On February 25, 1969, 36 U.S. Marines were killed by the North Vietnamese Army, who raided their base camp near the demilitarized zone.

On March 4, President Nixon threatened to resume bombing North Vietnam in retaliation for those Viet Cong attacks in the south. On March 15, U.S. troops went on the offensive inside the demilitarized zone. Two days later, President Nixon authorized Operation Menu, the secret bombing of Cambodia by B-52s, targeting North Vietnamese supply sanctuaries located along the border of Vietnam. But by this time, Sheldon was on his way home.

For the duration of Sheldon's tour, contact with friends and family at home was vital to his psychological well-being. One sleepless night he decided to write a letter to his father. In that letter he said that if his dad had taken all the money he spent on the education for Sheldon and his brothers and invested it, he would be a wealthy man today. His father later wrote back and said that he did invest the money and he was a wealthy man. After all, two of his sons were doctors and the other was a lawyer. "That's true love, isn't it?" said Sheldon.[163]

Many friends and family wrote to Sheldon while he was in Vietnam. Some days he would get a letter or two and some days he would get a mountain of letters because mail was not delivered regularly. Sheldon's father wrote to him every day. His brothers, Jack and Harold, wrote occasionally. Sheldon also mentioned with pride that every other week he would receive a letter from his high school football coach, Bobby Wilson. The coach's advice was "Keep your damn head down." His boyhood friend from Montgomery, Bart Starr, wrote to him a couple of times as did doctors he knew from Vandenberg Air Force Base, his parents' friends, relatives, friends from medical school, and his mom. In April 1968, Sheldon received a letter from Uncle Eugene, the man who had been estranged from Sheldon's family because of his support of civil rights. Critically important were letters from his wife. "She was my umbilical cord," he remarked. Packages and letters from home boosted his morale.[164]

Bart Starr's letter is a true expression of how folks at home were deeply moved by the commitment made by those serving in Vietnam.

Sheldon wrote to his wife every day and on several occasions made tapes for her as well. In one letter dated May 1, 1968, he stated, "I am enclosing a little map of the area to show you what the layout is here." He also sent letters to his mom and dad every day and to other friends and family members at times. Looking to the future, Sheldon also wrote to Dr. Stander, chairman of the Department of OB-GYN at the University of Cincinnati, regarding his residency at the hospital there after his discharge from the service. These activities bolstered his mental state.

Although Sheldon's time off was limited, he used it to de-stress himself. The team usually worked half a day on Sundays and would find time to relax in the afternoon. For Sheldon, this took the form of playing tennis not far from the compound.

The only relaxation that Sheldon enjoyed more than photography
was the tennis court on the grounds of the nearby convent.

Ned Jenkins and Sheldon with their 35mm cameras

Typical Cessna "Bird Dog" plane flown by Ned Jenkins

On May 1, 1968, May Day, a South Vietnamese holiday, Sheldon wrote to his wife that "because of the holiday, we did not work, and so I played tennis until about 1:30 p.m., got a haircut and slept for a couple of hours."[165]

Since Mac had a stereo in their room, Sheldon often listened to music. He also had reading material such as *Stars and Stripes, the Montgomery Advertiser* (sent by his father), *Time*, and the *New Yorker* magazine for his enjoyment. He kept up with current events and even commented on the presidential campaign in a letter to his wife:

> The death of Robert Kennedy certainly put a damper on what started out to be a very energetic campaign. I don't think there is much doubt that all this campaigning will lead to a final decision between Humphrey and Nixon. I would be highly surprised to see one of the "Peace Candidates," McCarthy or Rockefeller slip into their party's nomination. At any rate, I am supporting Nixon. I feel that he is the only man who can get us out of Vietnam in an honorable way. I want to get out of here but I'd like to do it with some sort of victory. I think Nixon can come closest to accomplishing this.[166]

Sheldon remarked that he enjoyed conversations with Don Ackerman, a civilian who worked with the border patrol in El Paso, Texas, and came to Vietnam to advise local police officials on how to fight the terrorist techniques used by the Viet Cong. Sheldon also spent time playing tennis with Ray Brewer, the ophthalmologist who had come to Vinh Long as part of the Volunteer Physicians in Vietnam Program. He told his wife that he hated to see Ray go. "One can certainly make some good friends over here, so that's one thing Vietnam is good for."[167]

The airfield had an officer's club that served dinner. The compound had a bar upstairs that was a hangout for them. He enjoyed an occasional beer, talking with colleagues, and playing cards, usually poker. Fred was often there playing poker with several corpsmen. The officers fraternized with enlisted men.

In addition, they frequently showed old movies there. Sheldon remarked, "They showed Dr. Zhivago ten times or more. Every time you turned around, there was Dr. Zhivago."[168] About once a quarter a live show would come to the area as well. At times Sheldon and his colleagues would eat at a local restaurant, and a place called Long Chou was a favorite choice. Typical Vietnamese food consisted of boiled fish, which was covered with an awful-smelling sauce called nuoc mam (made of fermented anchovies, among other things), or shrimp chips, which were almost like eating potato chips. However, the group would only go there under security guard.[169]

From time to time, parties took place to break up their routine. Several parties were held between the American and Vietnamese staff. In a tape he sent his wife, Sheldon talked about having a Christmas party. He also wrote about it in a letter: "We are having a MILPHAP Christmas Party tomorrow night, but I must say that it is quite difficult to get the real Christmas spirit over here. Vietnam just isn't very Christmassy."[170] Shortly after, on Christmas day, he wrote,

> I spent Christmas making rounds at the hospital this morning and then playing tennis for about 3 hours this morning. Then we had a Christmas dinner this afternoon followed by a few drinks. Presently there is a band upstairs supplying music for the party tonight. Everyone has spent the

entire day daydreaming about home. Maybe next year let's hope. How did you spend your Christmas?[171]

On Valentine's Day 1969, he noted, "There are all kinds of parties going on around here in celebration of the Tet New Year. I have not attended any of them and I don't intend to." The first day of Tet was February 17—the parties began earlier—and as of that date Sheldon had only 19 days remaining in Vietnam. He did not want to take any chances.[172]

Celebrations also took place to honor those going back to the States. For example, in a letter, Sheldon told his wife, "This afternoon we are having a going away party for Ray [Brewer] who is leaving in the a.m."[173]

Another way Sheldon relaxed was by taking pictures with the camera he bought in Tokyo in September 1968 when he served as a medical attendant on a hospital plane that took wounded soldiers to Japan. Sheldon sometimes flew with Forward Air Patrol pilot Ned Jenkins, who had his wife's name, Jeanie, painted on the plane, and they would go take photographs together.

In December 1968 Sheldon and Mac drove all over Vinh Long and took pictures. Such activities served to soften the reality of war. In one letter to his wife, written a month after his road trip with Mac, Sheldon remarked, "We have been spending some of our free time taking pictures. As I am sure you have gathered, I am really having a ball with the camera. I am accumulating a rather nice collection of slides."[174]

Sheldon did have leave time, and on his first wedding anniversary—November 26, 1968—he was able to meet his wife in Hawaii for two weeks. He brought along the pearls he had bought on a short trip to Japan. They stayed at the Illikai Hotel in Honolulu. Other than a visit to Pearl Harbor, they remained at the hotel and relaxed on the beach. Enjoying a good meal and catching up on his sleep were priorities for Sheldon. "It was hard to go back after that," he noted.[175]

These fun activities kept Sheldon going. He was looking to the future, to the time when he would be in the United States again and be reunited with his wife. He was looking forward to finishing his military duty and to finishing his residency program, so that he could begin his career as a doctor, start a family, and live the American dream.

8

Back to the States

I figure I have about 22 days left in Vinh Long City.

There are all kinds of parties going on around here in celebration of the Tet New Year.

I have not attended any of them and I don't intend to. I have the rest of my life to party.

Captain Sheldon Kushner, MD, February 1969

When Sheldon's tour of duty ended in March 1969, he left behind his colleagues, Mac and Fred. "Today [March 2, 1969] I am beginning my last week here in Vinh Long," Sheldon wrote his wife, and "in exactly one week I will be leaving here and in exactly two weeks I will be home with you."[176] Counting the days was a habit he had kept up throughout his tour.

Sheldon was granted a 30-day leave at the end of the tour, before having to report to his next assignment at Patrick Air Force Base near Cocoa Beach, Florida. He was required to take a route home that involved several plane rides, with the first leg of the homebound journey being Saigon to Travis Air Force Base in San Francisco. Sadly, after having given so much of himself trying to save the victims of the war, Sheldon was subjected to harassment by antiwar activists when he arrived at the airport in San Francisco, where they cursed him and spit on him. He felt demoralized.[177]

His next flight stopped in Texas before landing in Birmingham, Alabama, where his wife's apartment was located. While in Birmingham, he visited Dr. Walter Fromeyer, chairman of the Department of Internal Medicine at the University of Alabama Medical School. While in Vietnam, Sheldon had corresponded with Dr. Fromeyer about setting up his residency program.

From Birmingham, he and Carol drove south about 95 miles to his parents' house in Montgomery. The first thing his mother did was to take him out and buy him a new suit! He felt the warmth of those who had missed him while on tour—his insurance agent, Fred

Miller, even offered to treat him to dinner at any restaurant. Sheldon used the opportunity to enjoy one of his favorite foods, catfish.

During the month's leave when Sheldon and Carol were staying at Sheldon's childhood home, a package arrived from Jackie Ventura, one of the nurses he worked with at the hospital in Vinh Long. It contained a vase from Vietnam with flowers in it and a note that read, "Sorry I missed you."[178] Unfortunately, she had been out of town when Sheldon left for Saigon, and this was her kind way of saying good-bye. With a few precious days left before his leave ended, Sheldon and Carol vacationed in the Florida panhandle and spent time in New Orleans, where they met up with Dr. Ray Brewer, the ophthalmologist from Houston who had served with Sheldon for several months in Vinh Long.

The couple drove south into Central Florida, where Sheldon spent the last six months of his required time in the service at Patrick Air Force Base, a beautiful ocean-side location near the Atlantic. Here he served as a general medical officer, which was quite a change from his duty in Vinh Long. He worked a typical nine-to-five workday. The couple rented an apartment near the base. "Life was good," Sheldon remembered.[179] During his time at the base in 1969, Mac came to visit. They had an opportunity to swap stories and remember their time in Vietnam. At another time, while at Patrick, Sheldon was asked by the medical people to provide a slide show about his surgical experience in Vinh Long. Sheldon recalled that "it was well received."[180] This was a vast difference from the "welcome mat" at the airport in San Francisco.

Upon completion of his service at Patrick Air Force Base in September 1969, Sheldon began a three-year residency at Cincinnati General Hospital, in Ohio, a large facility with about 900 beds. Prior to his arrival, the city had experienced racial unrest and rioting in Avondale, a neighborhood in Cincinnati, after the assassination of civil rights leader Martin Luther King Jr. in April 1968. A mob smashed store windows, looted the stores, and burned merchandise. The Ohio National Guard was called to restore peace, but two people were killed, at least 220 were injured, and 260 were arrested during two nights of violence.

Such was the climate of the city where Sheldon spent the next few years. He had applied for the residency in January 1968 and had completed an interview for this residency with Dr. Richard Stander before going to Vietnam. Sheldon explained, "I had a wonderful residency under his direction and enjoyed a great relationship with my fellow residents and with the entire obstetrics and gynecology faculty." This wasn't the case with faculty members in other specialties and with the local private physicians, who were critical of his participation in the Vietnam War.[181]

Most of his OB-GYN patients in Cincinnati were young, black indigent women. He discovered that many of these women had boyfriends who were Black Panther members. For about six months, because of his southern accent and skin color, Sheldon was cursed at and spit on, and he received threats from the Panthers against his life and his family. He told his wife that he had to get out of there because he could not stand working under these conditions any longer. She worked nearby at Cincinnati's Christ Hospital as a nurse.

Less than a year later, when they were able to take a week off, the Kushners drove up to Wisconsin to be with relatives. As they were driving to Wisconsin from Ohio, the May 1970 Kent State murders occurred.[182] In addition to relatives, Sheldon and Carol visited his boyhood friend, Bart Starr. Sheldon shared with Bart the problems he was having back in Cincinnati and confided that he was seriously thinking of leaving the position. Bart told him it would be a big mistake to allow the ignorance and ugliness of some people to destroy his dreams. Sheldon thought about Bart's advice as they drove back to Cincinnati and decided he was right. So Sheldon and Carol resumed their jobs, and he completed his residency. By the end of his residency, the threats lessened. Sheldon took his exams and became board certified in obstetrics and gynecology.

His residency in Cincinnati highlighted his struggle with PTSD, one result of his service in Vietnam:[183]

> When I was doing my residency in Cincinnati, I was on call at night. There was an area for us to sleep and I'd wake up, after screaming nightmares. One of the surgeon residents told me: "we don't know what you're talking about. I'd appreciate it if you could sleep somewhere else." After that I was embarrassed to go to sleep. It has lasted to this day.[184]

The Kushners started a family in Cincinnati when, in October 1971, their daughter, Andrea Lynn, was born in Christ Hospital and was delivered by one of Sheldon's teachers, Dr. Robert Johnstone. Carol then left her nursing position at that hospital to care for Andrea. With Sheldon's internship completed, the Kushners left the area in September of 1972, and Sheldon began his medical career.

At first, Sheldon practiced medicine in Meridian, Mississippi, a city near the Alabama state line. He was one of three doctors in a small practice; the others were Dr. William Moore and Dr. W. H. Abraham. While a resident, Sheldon had visited Meridian to see Dr. Jim Pittman, a surgeon he had befriended while at Patrick Air Force Base. It was Jim who introduced him to his future colleagues William Moore and W. H. Abraham.

In 1975, Sheldon received a surprise package in the mail with no return address. He opened it and found his Star of David necklace. No note was in the package. When he was young, Sheldon received this necklace from his father, and he had worn it every day. One night he had left it near his bedside at the compound in Vinh Long, and it had vanished after he left his room during the second offensive in August 1968. He was grateful and amazed that this prized possession had been returned to him.

Andrea Lynn Kushner was joined by a little brother, Stephen Allen, who was born in Meridian in March 1975.[185] Within a year, job and family brought the Kushners back to Birmingham, where Carol's family lived and where Sheldon's brother Harold practiced law. East End Hospital had recruited Sheldon to utilize their facilities, although he had his own thriving practice as well. Brookwood Hospital in Birmingham also granted privileges to Sheldon, and he added two former medical school classmates to his private practice to help with the increasing patient load.

While there, Sheldon found out that Sebastian River Medical Center, in Sebastian, Florida, was looking for someone to head the Obstetrics Department. Having been stationed at Patrick Air Force Base, about an hour north of Sebastian, Sheldon was somewhat familiar with the area, with its palm trees, beaches, and mild tropical climate. It was very appealing. Although he regretted leaving many friends and his brother, Sheldon was eager to accept this new challenge.

In 1982 the Kushners moved to Vero Beach, and Sheldon set up a practice 20 minutes away in a medical building on the south side of Sebastian River Medical Center. Sheldon opened the Obstetrics Department at Sebastian in 1984, and while he headed that group, he was also on the board of the hospital for a short time, helping to hire and train the nurses for the unit and to obtain equipment needed for the ward. Soon he brought in a partner to his practice, Dr. Jane Henderson.

Sheldon enjoys retelling the story of the opening ceremony to dedicate the Sebastian River Medical Center obstetrics and substance abuse wards. It was to be a big event for the town. A tent was put up near U.S. 1, the main road in front of the hospital, and the guest speaker was Senator Bill Nelson from Florida. Many chairs were placed under the tent to accommodate the important invited guests. Sheldon described a memorable and unexpected episode that followed: "When Bill Nelson got up to speak, his seat in the front row was vacant, and after a few minutes, we noticed an elderly homeless man had walked over to the tent and sat down in the empty seat. It was a funny scene. I guess the hospital was meant to serve everyone."[186] To this day, Sheldon chuckles at how much more he recalls about that incident than about the words spoken by the invited guests.

Sheldon also served as chairman of the academic programs at the hospital. For one of the programs, he invited his old professor, Dr. Holt McDowell, to discuss carotid artery disease. The lecture was well received by all of his colleagues.

By the late 1980s, Sheldon decided to establish a private gynecological practice closer to home in Vero Beach, with Dr. Ernie Jackson. He became affiliated with the nearby Indian River Hospital, now called Indian River Medical Center

Soon another opportunity presented itself. In 1989, the family moved to Pensacola, Florida, and Sheldon became the associate director and chief of the Department of Gynecology at the Northwest Florida Residency Program in Obstetrics and Gynecology, Inc. This program was affiliated with the Tulane University and later affiliated with the University of Florida College of Medicine. Sheldon held associate clinical professor appointments at both schools. He taught surgery in at Sacred Heart Hospital in Pensacola, along with Dr. Louis Stalmaker, the director. They were also partners in a private practice there.

By the early 1990s Sheldon and Carol divorced, and Sheldon moved to Marathon in the Florida Keys after he learned that there was a critical need for a gynecologist. He practiced gynecology at Fisherman's Hospital from 1992 to 1995, and he served as the chief of staff; as such, Sheldon was responsible for the actions of the other doctors and the liaison between them and the hospital's administration. He held the position for about six months after which he retired because he developed incapacitating heart disease. Sheldon returned to Vero Beach and there he was able to take care of his mother, who had been living there since his father passed away in 1995. While in Vero, Sheldon met Lynn, who later became his wife. Lynn and her late husband, had relocated from their home in Connecticut, but he soon passed away after a short time in Florida when he became very ill. Sheldon realized how important she would be in his life as she helped him care for his mother and face new challenges.

Over the years, while patient care and surgery were his primary medical duties, Sheldon spoke to doctors, civics groups, and high school students on a variety of topics that reflected problems he saw firsthand in his practice: domestic violence, teen pregnancy, contraception, sexually transmitted diseases, health-threatening behaviors in teens, AIDS, hormone replacement therapy, and cancer screening. "The teen pregnancy rate in the United States is extremely high relative to what is seen in other industrialized countries. Our rates have decreased somewhat in recent years, but they are still too high and this problem remains a national embarrassment," explained Sheldon. "The consequences of teen pregnancy are devastating and the cost is staggering. As an obstetrician gynecologist, I felt that I had a responsibility to talk with young people and to adults about life threatening behaviors in teens."[187] Most of these speaking engagements were located in his county of residence, Indian River, as well as other nearby counties in South Florida: Brevard, St. Lucie, Palm Beach, Broward, Dade, and Monroe.

During the late 1990s, Sheldon also began teaching anatomy and physiology at Indian River State College, where he provided students with the practical application of the scientific information in his courses. Most of his students were nursing majors whom he felt would appreciate his brand of medical instruction given his experience in Vietnam.

While teaching as an adjunct professor, a friend from medical school, Dr. Betty Ruth, called him about a position in Greenville, Alabama, a community of about 10,000 people south of Montgomery. She wanted him to come there to serve in a private clinic because she knew that his background would be a good fit at this location, which was a federally designated area of critical need. At this time, his heart problems were stable, so in 2009, Sheldon and Lynn relocated to Greenville for about 18 months and witnessed many health issues in that community.

Many of his patients were young black girls who weighed up to 300 pounds. Many others were pregnant, and venereal disease was widespread. Parental guidance was lacking, and the school systems were underfunded and substandard. The federal regulations with Medicare and Medicaid stifled his progress to provide good care for these patients. In time, though, the position in Greenville resulted in a recurrence of his heart problems, making it necessary to leave that work and return to Vero Beach, Florida, in 2011, where he resumed teaching anatomy and physiology at the college and participated as a school board member at the nearby Indian River Charter High School until he retired in December 2015. Shortly after, Sheldon and Lynn moved to Point Clear, Alabama.

Sheldon's time in Greenville reflected his philosophy of care: "I've always considered myself a right-wing conservative with a social conscience. I took care of people even though they couldn't afford to pay me. I took care of them no matter what."[188] His education, internship, service in Vinh Long, and residency had prepared him well for his practice of medicine in Mississippi, Alabama, and Florida, and his time in the States provided a perspective on the purposes of the Vietnam War and gave him pause to consider what that war meant in his own life.

9

Final Thoughts of a Veteran Surgeon

We did a lot of surgery and saved a lot of people's lives.
We filled a great humanitarian need.

Dr. Sheldon Kushner, MD, Interview 2014

Sheldon's tour in Vietnam left its mark on him. In many ways the experience made him a prisoner of that war. The psychological and emotional walls that his service in Vietnam created have been difficult to overcome. He returned to the United States a changed man.

Like many other veterans, Sheldon's year of service as a surgeon gave him a whole new perspective about the Vietnam War. He saw the horror of war every day as he treated wounded and fatally injured civilians in Vinh Long. The sounds and smells made a lasting impression on him. He explained, "I think I've had enough of war for a lifetime."[189] "I came back quite different than when I went over there. . . . When I first went over there I was ready to lead the troops over the hill to kill the Viet Cong. I was a believer in the domino theory."[190] Sheldon was truly a war hawk, committed to making a difference in South Vietnam because he feared that if one country were taken by an expansionist communist neighbor, others nearby would also fall.

Sheldon was upset that our military ended up injuring and killing so many Vietnamese civilians. Even though Forward Air Control pilots marked targets with white phosphorus, the subsequent air strikes often resulted in many civilian casualties outside the marked area.

He was also upset that the United States was supporting the South Vietnamese government. "They mistreated their own people," he noted. "We were supporting a corrupt and inept government of South Vietnam. They were interested in taking our money and supplies and selling them. I can't prove it, but stuff sent to us that was used for medical care never got to us—it was sold off."[191] From working with a Vietnamese doctor in the hospital, Sheldon concluded that this doctor did not want to learn about American medicine and did not place the same value on human life as American doctors did. One of Sheldon's medics, Tom Graue, reaffirmed Sheldon's feelings: "The Vietnamese doctor was money hungry and interested in making money, not in helping patients."[192]

Even before he came home, Sheldon was questioning America's role in Vietnam. After just two months in country, he expressed his feelings about the war to his wife: "I think we should let these people handle their own problems."[193] In a message he recorded on tape for her, Sheldon said, "I think we ought to get the hell out of here especially if we are not going to win this war."[194] In a letter to his father almost halfway through his tour, Sheldon expressed his feelings about the war: "I guess I just can't understand this war. I don't understand why we are here and why all these people are dying. I don't even know who they are. I know there is someone, somewhere, who has his reasons for all this."[195] After learning about the Pueblo crew being released,[196] Sheldon continued to reflect on the war: "I was certainly glad to hear that the Pueblo crew is going to be released. Now I just wish that we could bring an end to this awful war over here."[197]

For Sheldon, it was his direct involvement in the daily crisis the innocent civilians faced that made him less the war hawk than the humanitarian surgeon:

> I can't seem to forget the tragedy and the faces of so many injured and killed women and children and older people. I also can't forget the faces of so many young kids who gave so much for something I am sure they never understood either. . . . No one knows what Agent Orange did to the civilian population and what genetic defects are carried forth by the population.[198]

He realized that many in the military wanted the war to continue because it provided a means of promotion for the officers. From his reading about Vietnam since returning to the States, Sheldon made this observation: "President Johnson was lied to by (Robert) MacNamara and by General (William) Westmoreland. They would say, we just need more money and more troops and we can win this war."[199]

Finally, Sheldon feels bitter about being put in the situation of having to take care of the injured with limited training and limited resources. "I know I made mistakes because I did not have the training and I can't forget that," he remarked. "The government should have drafted a general surgeon who had several years of experience. They should have done it right!" He added, "I was right out of internship and here I was doing blood vessel work and major abdominal surgery and craniotomies and major orthopedic work, and I should not have been in this position." He often thinks about the patients he could not help, due to his lack of expertise and experience.[200]

In June of 2015, Sheldon traveled to Los Angeles to meet Mac, his former roommate and physician colleague at the hospital in Vinh Long. They had a wonderful reunion and shared the joys and sorrows of their time in Vinh Long. Over the years, Sheldon kept in contact with Mac, who currently lives in Southern California, not far from Sheldon's daughter. Like other veterans, Sheldon developed close ties with the people he served with in Vietnam.

Despite Sheldon's feeling that the war lacked clear objectives, he has a special sense of pride regarding what he and his medical team accomplished: "We did a lot of surgery and saved a lot of people's lives. We filled a great humanitarian need."[201]

Time for old friends; Dr. Sheldon Kushner (L) and Dr. James (Mac) McComb (R)
on a trip to Los Angeles

Sheldon in retirement, speaking to a group about health care and politics

Epilogue

When considering the experiences that suggested a book title about "trauma and tenacity," I found three writings penned by Dr. Sheldon Kushner, at various times in his life, that could be read independently from this book and still convey the message of a man completely dedicated to his profession and the care of people. One was a letter written to his father, "Pop," from Vietnam in 1968; in it, Sheldon expressed his frustration with the war and assured his father that he was safe and would soon be home. Sheldon also sent a letter to Colonel David Hackworth,[202] a veteran of many wars, in which he expressed his thanks for a book the colonel had published in 2002 titled Steel My Soldiers' Hearts. In his letter, Sheldon explained what the book meant to him and how he felt about his own experience in war.[203] The last writing is an acknowledgment in which Sheldon conveyed his deep conviction that without the others on his team in Vinh Long, his work would not have been possible.

— Mary Jane Ingui, PhD

AUGUST 8, 1968

LETTER TO POP, SHELDON'S FATHER

Dear Pop,

It is now 11:00 p.m. and Mac and I have just returned to the compound after spending one hell of a day in the operating room. As I am sure you have been reading in the paper, we are in the middle of the so-called Second Offensive by the V.C. The war is almost as intense now as it was during the Tet Offensive in January. The injured patients are pouring in and we simply cannot even put a dent into what really needs to be done.

It is frustrating to be unable to help everyone. It is also frustrating to not have the proper training to provide the type of care that some of these people need. Our government doesn't seem to care that Mac and I are not trained surgeons. They only seem to care that there are two doctors in Vinh Long Province providing care to the wounded civilians. It is almost like they consider these people as something less than real people. I can say with authority that these are real people like you and I. They have feelings, they hurt, they bleed and they die just like us. They all have someone who loves them just like us.

As you can tell, I am a little down right now. It seems that life is nothing but blood and guts and broken bones and earth. I can't believe that there are any boundaries, or any political concepts that could possibly be worth all of this Pop. I am sure that if the people at home understood what was really going on over there, they would never tolerate this war. I keep wondering how many more people have to die before it will be decided that we have accomplished whatever it is that we are trying to accomplish.

Pop, I am really OK and in spite of the intensity of the war, I am safe. I guess I just can't understand this war. I don't understand why we are here and why all these people are dying. I don't even know who they are. I know that there is someone somewhere who has his reasons for all this. I can accept that, but I guess some time I just get tired and depressed, and I am just not as strong as I need to be.

I know that the war is harder for you than for me. However, Jack is home now, and my tour of duty is more than half over. I know that I am not alone and that soon I will be able to come home. I just hope that no one in our family will ever again have to experience the overwhelming shame and horror of war, please God.

Love, Sheldon
P.S. I love you Pop

APRIL 2002

LETTER TO COLONEL DAVID HACKWORTH

Colonel David Hackworth:

From March 1968 to March 1969 I worked as a general surgeon in Vinh Long, not terribly far from Dong Tam. I was with a MILPHAP unit attached to the MACV unit in Vinh Long. My main function was to take care of Vietnamese civilians who got injured and to provide medical support to the MACV team with whom I was living. I burned out on trauma surgery and went into obstetrics and gynecology when I returned from Vietnam.

I never really understood that war and I can't seem to forget the tragedy and the faces of so many injured and killed women and children and older people. I also can't forget the faces of so many of our young kids who gave so much for something I am sure they never understood either.

Your book is excellent as it serves to remember so many of our brave young people who lived and died in a horribly difficult situation. I congratulate you for a well written book and especially for your unselfish efforts in Vietnam.

Without your leadership and dedication, we would have certainly lost many more precious people. Thanks for sharing your insights and this part of your life with us.

Sincerely,
Sheldon R. Kushner, MD

FEBRUARY 3, 2017

THANK YOU TO THOSE WITH WHOM I SERVED

My final thoughts to those with whom I served;
The MILPHAP Team #558 was successful in providing much needed medical
assistance to the Vietnamese population in Vinh Long because of the untiring
efforts of some very special people. I am proud to have been part of this team,
and the following individuals have my deep appreciation for all they did.
I will never forget the individuals who gave so much to help a suffering
population that was severely victimized by a war that most of us have
never understood.

Dr. James Gordon McComb was my roommate and my medical partner for
the time I served in Vietnam. Mac, as he was known to me, provided excellent
medical judgment that was extremely helpful to me. Mac and I inspired
each other and learned from each other. His conscientious attitude and his
humanitarian drive were a major part in the way this team functioned.
Mac is now a pediatric neurosurgeon on the faculty of the University of
Southern California School of Medicine in Los Angeles, California, where
he also is in private practice. Since our time in Vietnam, our medical careers
developed in different directions, but I know of no colleague whom I have
admired and respected more.

Dr. Fred Seaman provided quality pediatric care to many children in
Vinh Long Province, where this level of medical care had never been available.
Doctor Seaman was the commander of the MILPHAP Team and he provided
mature leadership in addition to the pediatric care. After leaving Vietnam,
Doctor Seaman entered private pediatric practice. I will always be grateful
for his contribution to our efforts in Vinh Long.

I feel much appreciation for the efforts of the medical corpsmen who gave so much of themselves to help this large population of injured Vietnamese people. Thomas Graue, Titus Herr, Jim Gates, Don Schluter, Robby Robinson, Bill Grover, Gary Kohler, Sandy Sanchez, and Jeff Purtle are all special individuals, and we could never have done what we did without them.

Corpsman Smith, who we called Smitty, and Lieutenant Howard Hersey provided administrative support that was extremely helpful and appreciated. Jackie Ventura and Marcella O'Connor were American registered nurses who worked with us on a special nonmilitary program. Their help and their caring efforts were invaluable.

Dr. Loran Morgan from Torrington, Wyoming, and Dr. Ray Brewer from Houston, Texas, were civilian ophthalmologists who volunteered three months of their time to treat Vietnamese patients with eye problems. They were with the Volunteer Physicians Vietnam program and they made major contributions that were very much appreciated.

Thanks to all of you for your dedication and service.

Appendix:
Letters Home from Vietnam

Dr. Sheldon Kushner's Letters Home from Vietnam and Current Events in the United States

The letters written by Dr. Sheldon Kushner, combined with reel-to-reel tapes, photographs, and his current recollections, provide the basis for this biographical snapshot of a surgeon's life in Vietnam from March 1968 to March 1969. These letters are presented here for a firsthand experience of his tour of duty in Vinh Long. I have also included stateside events that occurred on the same day or within a few days of Sheldon's writing a letter, in order to give the reader a place in time for each letter. In this way, the reader can see what was happening in America on those days that Sheldon was corresponding with his wife and family while he was wholly engaged in serving his country in Vietnam. Gaps in any letter or days missing in the year of service, can be attributed to very personal words to Sheldon's wife, Carol, and were removed out of respect for his family.

— Mary Jane Ingui, PhD

March 1968

MARCH 22, VIETNAM

Dear Carol,
I am now in a MACV hotel compound in Saigon. I will
stay here for about three days after which I will go on down
to Vinh Long. I spent my first night here at Tan Son Nhut
AFB. The base was hit heavily with mortar fire but I never
heard a sound, as I was so sound asleep. Last night I took
my first shower since leaving San Francisco and my second
shave. I felt like someone had just given me a million dollars.

Saigon is a most amazing place. I was immediately
overwhelmed by the filth, the smell, the crowded conditions,
and the traffic, which is unbelievable. The heat and humidity
are fierce, but not intolerable as yet as it does cool off at
night. I am definitely going to Vinh Long unless something
is changed in the next three days. From all I can gather, this
has been a relatively safe place so far. I certainly hope that it
remains so.

JOHNSON ORDERED OFF CAR

March 22, San Francisco, CA: Lyndon Johnson was ordered off a San Francisco cable car for eating an ice cream cone while riding the system.

NUCLEAR TEST COMPLETED

March 22, Nevada: It was reported that 10 days ago, around March 12th, the United States performed a nuclear test at a Nevada test site.

ROCKEFELLER WILL NOT RUN FOR PRESIDENT

March 22, New York, NY: Potential Republican presidential candidate, Nelson Rockefeller, has saddened his GOP supporters by announcing he will not run for President. He did leave hope by saying he would accept the nomination if he were drafted at the convention. He will continue though to speak out about the issues.

| LETTERS HOME FROM VIETNAM | CURRENT EVENTS |

MARCH 23, VIETNAM

Dear Carol,

Just a note to tell you I am doing o.k. and that I love you very much. I am still at MACV headquarters, and I am scheduled to go to Vinh Long on Monday the 25th or on the 26th. I am still getting briefings here, some comforting and some very disturbing, but all and all I am doing fine, maybe a little scared, but otherwise OK. I have been unable to come by any electricity as of yet, so I will complete my tape when I get to Vinh Long.

MARCH 30, VIETNAM

Dear Carol,

The Vietnamese are very nice people, but they can really frustrate the hell out of you. . . . Their lunch break every day is from 12:00 noon until 2:30 p.m. They usually start late and quit early. They do not want you to advise them (which is what we are supposed to be doing). They want you to do the work for them and they want you to do it their way. Can you imagine that?? . . . Charlie or the V.C., are well trained and hard working. If we were to leave, this place would belong to Charlie over night.

FIRST DELEGATE NAMED TO CONGRESS

March 23, Washington, DC: Rev. Walter Fauntroy was named the first nonvoting congressional delegate from Washington, DC.

COHEN STUDYING GUARANTEED WAGE

March 23, Washington DC: Wilbur J. Cohen, President Johnson's nominee to be Secretary of Health, Education and Welfare, raised the possibility today of tying the nation's welfare system to some form of payroll tax to overcome American disdain about "handouts." He is part of a commission looking at a guaranteed wage and a regressive income tax for welfare cases.

JOHNSON TO TALK TO NATION TOMORROW NIGHT ON VIETNAM WAR

March 30, Washington, DC: President Johnson will address the nation to deal "rather fully" with the situation in Vietnam, including further troop build-ups, the possibility of reserve call-ups, and the additional costs associated with these changes.

JOHNSON NOT TO SEEK ANOTHER TERM

March 31, Washington, DC: Lyndon B. Johnson made headlines with the shocking announcement he would not seek reelection to become president of the United States.

April 1968

APRIL 4, VIETNAM

Dear Carol,
The high military officials here seem to think a peace is going to be negotiated in the next few months. This will not in any way shorten my stay here. They have made it clear to us that the advisory teams will stay. But I would rather be here during a peace rather than during a war.

You will never believe what I am doing now. The colonel has decided that there are too many GIs in the area with Gonorrhea. So, he has selected yours truly to run a special clinic for all the Vietnamese prostitutes to try to eliminate the disease as much as possible. So one day I can tell our children that their daddy went to war in Vietnam to fight the G.C., while everyone else was fighting the V.C.

APRIL 5, VIETNAM

Dear Carol,
I was quite disturbed today to hear about Martin Luther King. I am quite fearful of the consequences. You be careful, you hear me?

MLK SHOT DEAD IN MEMPHIS

April 4, Memphis, TN: The Rev. Dr. Martin Luther King Jr. was shot and killed. The incident occurred at the Lorraine Motel in Memphis, from one round of a 3006 rifle. The alleged assassin wielding the weapon was James Earl Ray.

JOHNSON DELAYS TRIP TO HAWAII

April 4, Washington, DC: President Johnson postponed his trip to Hawaii for a Vietnam strategy meeting with top military leaders. He may leave by tomorrow. This decision came after he heard of the death of the Rev. Dr. Martin Luther King Jr.

TERRENCE COOK INSTALLED AS NYC ARCHBISHOP WHILE RIOTING CONTINUED

April 5, New York, NY: The Most Rev. Terrence Cook was installed as archbishop of New York as President Johnson looked on at St. Patrick's Cathedral.

Despite the hope for calm, violence and rioting in U.S. cities followed the assassination of Dr. King.

LETTERS HOME FROM VIETNAM	CURRENT EVENTS

APRIL 6, VIETNAM

Dear Carol,

I am back in Vinh Long after spending a profitable morning in Can Tho. Myron Goodman let me use his jeep down there and I was able to get all my business done without difficulty. That boy has really been a help. I am staying quite busy, doing laparotomies, amputations, tendons and the works. Staying busy makes time go by. By the time you get this letter it will be almost one month.

APRIL 9, VIETNAM

Dear Carol,

We are busy as hell here. I can't get caught up with all the surgery I have to do. Honey, I spend all day operating, except at noon when I play tennis. Not really a bad life, but needless to say I would rather be at home with you. Last night we got quite a bit of mortar fire, but no harm done to us. The town however got zapped, thus I end up in surgery all day. Do you remember that loud thunder we heard? Well, multiply that by 10, and that is how loud these mortars sound when they come in.

SOLDIERS SENT TO WASHINGTON, DC, AND CHICAGO AFTER RIOTING

April 6, Washington, DC: President Johnson ordered troops into the Capitol and Chicago as Negro populations took to the streets after Dr. King's assassination. Many called it an "insurrection."

KING LAID TO REST

April 9, Atlanta, GA: The coffin of the Rev. Dr. Martin Luther King Jr. was carried through the streets of Atlanta on a crude farm wagon pulled by two Georgia mules. It was followed by tens of thousands of mourners, black and white, the average person mingling with the powerful, all in silent tribute to the slain Negro civil rights leader.

LETTERS HOME FROM VIETNAM   **CURRENT EVENTS**

APRIL 10, VIETNAM

Dear Carol,

Today the mail man didn't make it to Vinh Long, so I have been re-reading some of your letters I received yesterday and the day before. Today has been the worst day I have experienced here. The food here even though purchased in the U.S., can really make you sick as hell and today I got it. However, I am feeling better now and by the time you get this letter I am sure I will be a well man. Everybody here gets it regularly and it is just something you must learn to tolerate.

Today I became an orthopedic surgeon. For the first time in my life I opened up a knee joint and got a bullet out of it. Messy as hell, but I got the job done, I think.

I love all this talk I hear about peace talks. I doubt seriously if an end of fighting would bring me home sooner, but things would still be better.

APRIL 13, VIETNAM

Dear Carol,

I did an open reduction of a fractured humerus, repaired two Achilles tendons, drained an appendiceal abscess, and several other small procedures. So the day flew by and every day counts. Honey, that's one more out of the way.

Tonight MACV Advisory Team #52 is having a big party. They had dinner, which I went to.

ACADEMY AWARDS HELD

April 10, Hollywood, CA: The Academy Awards were held tonight instead of April 9. They were postponed due to the death and funeral of Dr. Martin Luther King Jr.

U.S. MILITARY RESERVES CALLED UP

April 11, Washington, DC: U.S. Secretary of Defense Clark Clifford called 24,500 military reserves to action for two-year commitments, and announced a new troop ceiling of 549,500 American soldiers in Vietnam.

CORE REVITALIZES ITS YOUTH GROUPS

April 13, Harlem, NY: The Congress of Racial Equality revitalized its youth group, the Students Congress of Racial Equality, as a result of the group's efforts to keep the streets of Harlem and Bedford-Stuyvesant peaceful during the recent disorders.

| LETTERS HOME FROM VIETNAM | CURRENT EVENTS |

APRIL 19, VIETNAM

Dear Carol,

Tomorrow morning, I am doing an open reduction on a fractured humerus and an appendicular abscess. Being an American Bac Si (Vietnamese for Doctor) is still a frustrating experience. My V.D. clinic is running right along, but I really don't know how much good I am doing. So far, 13 of 26 prostitutes have had a positive G.C. smear. I still think this is a futile effort though. But again it is something to do.

APRIL 26, VIETNAM

Dear Carol,

It is very late and I am very, very tired. I did three major operative procedures, plus many minor type procedures and I am absolutely exhausted.

APRIL 29, VIETNAM

Dear Carol,

Everything here is OK, except that I am busy as hell. I have been operating all day, every day this week and I am exhausted. Thank goodness tomorrow is a holiday.

CORNELL UNIVERSITY DISRUPTION BY ARMED BLACK STUDENTS

April 19, Ithaca, NY: Armed black students at Cornell University forcibly ejected parents and university employees from Willard Straight Hall and occupied it. Their complaint was that the university lacked a program relevant to black students.

200,000 DEMONSTRATE

April 26, New York, NY: More than 200,000 college and high school students in the metropolitan area cut classes during a student strike against the Vietnam War. The event was part of an International Day of Demonstrations.

NEGROES' BOYCOTT IN MISSISSIPPI GAINS MERCHANTS' CONCESSIONS

April 29, Greenwood, MS: A Negro boycott organized by clerics and run like a military campaign has crippled business in the Mississippi Delta town of Greenwood, forcing one group of white merchants to seek out the boycott leaders and make peace.

May 1968

MAY 1, VIETNAM

Dear Carol,

Today is May Day, a big South Vietnamese holiday and an even bigger communist holiday. Because of the holiday, we did not work, and so I played tennis until about 1:30 p.m., got a haircut and slept for a couple of hours.

I tried to get to Can Tho this a.m. to get my travel pay and per diem money. However, I couldn't get out of here all morning, so I gave up trying around 11 a.m. I probably would have gotten down there, but I could not have gotten back until tomorrow. Can Tho is a bad place to be under any circumstances at night, much less on a big communist holiday. The $25 is not worth that. However, I will try to get down there.

MAY 5, VIETNAM

Dear Carol,

I am enclosing a little map of the area to show you what the layout is here. There has been a definite increase in V.C. activities in this area. However, the V.C. in this area fight a guerilla war here consisting mainly of snipers, ambushes, and mortars. The mortars are the only thing I have to worry about.

This province like most provinces in Vietnam is entirely owned by Charlie at night, except for the town of Vinh Long. During the day, Charlie owns about half of the province. There are already about 1,500 American military personnel here. However, today we received 1,000 new men, which

PICKETERS CIRCLE COLUMBIA UNIVERSITY

May 1, New York, NY: Columbia University was ringed by hundreds of picketing students seeking to keep the institution paralyzed in the wake of a police raid that cleared demonstrators from five buildings they had occupied.

$1.5 BILLION TO BE SPENT ON CLEVELAND REDEVELOPMENT

May 1, Cleveland, OH: Plans for a 10-year $1.5-billion program to reconstruct and redevelop the entire city were announced by Mayor Carl B. Stokes.

HEART TRANSPLANTS A SUCCESS

May 5, Houston, TX: Two teams of surgeons at St. Luke's Hospital completed simultaneous heart and kidney transplant operations. Officials reported both patients were "doing well."

NAVY WILL PAY MORE

May 5, Washington, DC: With the approval of the Defense Department, General Electric and Westinghouse are being paid several hundred thousand dollars

is two air cavalry battalions. With them came 80 new helicopters. So the defense of the area is really building up. However, it's really going to be tough getting a tennis court now. I will write again tomorrow.

MAY 6, VIETNAM

Dear Carol,

Well another day is down and that is one less than yesterday, right? As you have probably read in the papers, the V.C. have started another nationwide offensive, certainly trying to gain bargaining power for the Paris peace talks which begin in 4 days. Here we received about 30–40 mortar rounds on the airfield Saturday night, all was quiet last night. Tonight everyone is ready and alert. Honey, let me assure you I am OK.

I am secure and very well protected. OK.

Today was unreal in surgery. I found myself wiring a jaw together of all things. Hell, I might be an oral surgeon one day.

more annually by the Navy than they would receive doing the same work for the Atomic Energy Commission.

LURLEEN WALLACE, ALABAMA GOVERNOR, IS DEAD OF CANCER

May 6, Montgomery, AL: Lurleen Burns Wallace (1926–1968) died from cancer a mere 16 months after taking office as governor of Alabama. Although she had clearly been elected as a stand-in for her husband, George Wallace, Alabamians genuinely mourned the loss of not only the first woman to be elected to the position but also someone with whom many of the state's average citizens could relate.

COLUMBIA REOPENING PICKETED

May 6, Manhattan, NY: Picketers marched outside a dozen classroom buildings on Columbia University's troubled campus in Manhattan in an attempt to dissuade teachers and students from entering even for informal discussions. A student organization (SDS) found documents that showed Columbia University was connected with the Vietnam War through weapons research. The picketing spilled into occupying buildings and closing the campus in protest to this involvement.

LETTERS HOME FROM VIETNAM   **CURRENT EVENTS**

MAY 7, VIETNAM

Dear Carol,

Things are continuing the same here. I am doing 2 to 3 to 4 major op cases a day and many, many minor procedures. It does tend to make the time go by. I still play tennis each day at noon, and by 9 or 10 p.m. I am usually flaked out.

MAY 12, VIETNAM

Dear Carol,

This morning some of our rangers demolished a couple of hundred V.C. who were lurking about the airfield. They described it as a good kill. War is awful, isn't it? Other than this, darling, there is nothing new here. I am still thinking about R + R and seeing you again. Two months are almost gone.

MAY 13, VIETNAM

Dear Carol,

One more day down and one more day closer to home. They all count. Today, I did 4 major op cases and I am exhausted. This afternoon, they brought in 14 9-year-old kids, whose school was blown up. 7 were dead and 1 died shortly. A sadder sight I don't believe I have ever seen. I just wish I knew more and that I could do more for these kids.

Well, today I weighed in at 162 lbs., 20 less than the day I arrived.

I'm back. I bet you didn't know I was gone. A V.C. sniper just opened fire on our house and he received in return about 250 rounds of M-16 fire. They brought him in to me and he actually looked like a big piece of hamburger meat. There was nothing I could do except tell everyone they could quit

MORTGAGE RATE TO INCREASE

May 7, Washington, DC: The interest rate on Government-backed home mortgages was raised to 6 3/4 from 6 per cent today, but the effective rate to buyers or sellers will hardly be increased.

MARCH OF THE POOR

May 12, Washington, DC: Led by Rev. Ralph Abernathy, the March of the Poor reached Washington, DC.

LENNON AND MCCARTNEY PROMOTE NEW COMPANY IN NYC

May 13, New York, NY: John Lennon and Paul McCartney promote their new company, Apple Corps Ltd., in New York City, giving interviews throughout the day, where they held a press conference at the Americana Hotel to announce the establishment of an American branch of the company.

firing. He was dead. 250 rounds to kill 1 V.C. The army estimates that it costs about $250,000 to kill 1 V.C. So our boys did pretty well. $250,000 to kill 1 V.C. For 1/250 of that we could probably talk the same guy into coming over to our side. Well that's it for tonight.

MAY 15, VIETNAM

Dear Carol,

I have received no letters for the past few days. The mail service is all fouled up right now because of the trouble in Saigon. The boys were telling me that during Tet they went 18 days without getting mail. I hope that doesn't happen to us. Other than the fact that I miss you very much, things are generally OK. The civilian casualties are still pouring in and we are operating like crazy. I'm sure I have done 10–12 major cases in the last 3 days. It's been a long time since I have been this tired.

CITY OF THE POOR BEGINS IN THE NATION'S CAPITAL

May 13, Washinton, DC: The Rev. Ralph David Abernathy today dedicated "Resurrection City, U. S. A.," with a vow "to plague the Pharaohs of this nation with plague after plague until they agree to give us meaningful jobs and a guaranteed annual income."

SEC. FOWLER SEEKS SPENDING CUTS

May 13, Washington, DC: Treasury Secretary Henry H. Fowler today became the first top Administration official to endorse publicly both the 10 per cent tax increase and the $6-billion in spending cuts worked out last week by Senate-House negotiators.

MCCARTHY PREDICTS A THREE-WAY DEMOCRATIC CONTEST

May 15, Washington, DC: Senator Eugene J. McCarthy of Minnesota said that the contest for the Democratic presidential nomination would be a three-way race right up to the party convention in Chicago in August.

LETTERS HOME FROM VIETNAM | **CURRENT EVENTS**

MAY 16, VIETNAM

Dear Carol,

The civilian casualties are still pouring in and I can't remember when I was tired as I am now. I am 100% exhausted. I have never seen so many badly injured people at one time. It does make the time go by however. I don't know exactly what is going on with the peace talks, but my feelings have not changed. Actually, my feelings have become stronger. I think we should let these people handle their own problems. They are so ungrateful it makes you want to cry.

MAY 17, VIETNAM

Dear Carol,

The civilian casualties are still pouring in so fast that it is absolutely unreal. The amount of surgery is just absolutely overwhelming. I just wish I knew more about surgery and I wish there were more of us. We are absolutely exhausted, but hopefully the V.C. will calm down a little.

This morning I was awakened by a noise like I have never heard before. The whole house was shaking and I thought the world was coming to an end. The noise was a B-52 strike about 15 miles away. I would hate to be on the receiving end of those things.

MASSACRE SHOCKS AMERICAN PUBLIC

May 16, New York, NY: Reports reached the American news media about the brutal killing of between 200 and 500 unarmed civilians at My Lai by a platoon of American soldiers. Air Force copter pilots placed themselves between the soldiers and the civilians to protect them and stop the massacre.

SUPREME COURT RULING

May 17, Washington, DC: The Supreme Court ruled that states cannot bar union picketing in a privately owned shopping center. Justice Thurgood Marshall explained in the 6–3 decision that the Court wanted to protect free expression, which was at the heart of the First Amendment.

MARCH OF THE POOR DELAYED DUE TO FINANCIAL PROBLEMS

May 17, Washington, DC: The national coordinator of the Poor People's Campaign today called on marchers and sympathizers not already on the way here aboard official bus caravans to delay their arrival until May 30 because the movement is in serious financial and managerial trouble.

LETTERS HOME FROM VIETNAM　　　　　　**CURRENT EVENTS**

MAY 23, VIETNAM

Dear Carol,
Hi Darling . . . It is 6:30 a.m. and I just woke up. I came in
last night at 8:00 p.m. so completely exhausted that I ate
supper and then just collapsed on the bed. I just wanted to
get this letter to you to tell you that I am OK.

MAY 24, VIETNAM

Dear Carol,
The OB-GYN journal hasn't arrived. I'm sure they will be
coming along soon. Guess what! There is another book we
need. It is a "Grant's Atlas of Anatomy." Would you send
this Darling? We all need it and I am pretty sure I have it. It
is a really big book. I have not received the OB book yet, but
I am sure that I soon will.

MAY 25, VIETNAM

Dear Carol,
I guess you are just about ready to leave. I also plan to drop
a line to the Smiths. All are really No. 1 people (over here to
the Vietnamese, everything is on a 10 scale. No. 1 is great;
No. 10 is the worst).

POLITICAL PRIMARIES ON BOTH SIDES OF THE AISLE

May 23, Nebraska: New York Senator Robert Kennedy won his second presidential primary, by getting 53 percent of the Democratic vote in Nebraska.

On the Republican side, Nixon won handily with 70 percent. Runners up on the Democrat side were McCarthy (31 percent); Humphrey (9 percent); Johnson (6 percent). On the Republican side, runners up were Reagan (22 percent); Rockefeller (5 percent)

TIME MAGAZINE COVER REVEALED

May 24, New York, NY: The cover of Time magazine featured the Democratic candidate for president, Robert Kennedy, along with a feature article about his candidacy.

ROBERT KENNEDY CALLS FOR GUN CONTROL

May 25, Roseburg, OR: Democratic presidential candidate Senator Robert F. Kennedy called for gun control in Roseburg, Oregon, the site of the nation's latest school massacre.

MAY 28, VIETNAM

Dear Carol,

Another day is down, and slowly but surely they will all go by. I count every single one. Today was another one of those very busy days. I did 3 major op procedures. Believe it or not it gets old. I really miss OB-GYN more than ever before. Honey, hold off on the Kistner Gyn book [Kistner's Gynecology: Principles and Practice]. I'll get one when I get back. I'm sure the OB book will keep me busy. However, I have not received it as of yet. I'm sure it will arrive soon.

Darling, all here is about the same as it has been. I do think the fighting may be letting up a little. I am busy reading the "Confessions of Nat Turner." I just decided to start over, as I forgot what the first part was about.

"MRS. ROBINSON" HITS THE AIRWAVES

May 28, New York, NY: Simon and Garfunkel's "Mrs. Robinson" hit the radio airwaves in America.

SENATOR MCCARTHY WINS UPSET OVER KENNEDY

May 28, Portland, Oregon: Senator Eugene J. McCarthy won a stunning upset victory over Senator Robert F. Kennedy in the Oregon Democratic primary. Some say that this spells a tough time ahead for Kennedy in the California primary.

THE SCORPION MAY BE LOST AT SEA

May 28, Washington, DC: A vast air-sea search for the missing nuclear-powered attack submarine Scorpion passed the 24-hour mark today with increasing signs of doubts that her 99-man crew would be found in time. The submarine was enroute back to its home base in Norfolk, Va, after exercises with the Sixth Fleet in the Mediterranean.

June 1968

LETTERS HOME FROM VIETNAM

CURRENT EVENTS

JUNE 1, VIETNAM

Dear Carol,

I'm sending this letter to you at home, because I don't think it will get to you in Dallas. Today seemed to start the cycle all over again as I did 4 major procedures and I think Mac did 4 or 5. Tomorrow is Sunday and I am looking forward to the rest and to a little tennis. My game was off today, so I need to work on it tomorrow.

HELEN KELLER, 87, DIES

June 1, Westport, CT: Helen Keller, who overcame blindness and deafness to become the symbol of the indomitable human spirit, passed away. She was living in Westport, Connecticut.

ROBERT KENNEDY SHOT

June 5, Los Angeles, CA: On the night of the California primary, Robert Kennedy addressed a large crowd of supporters at the Ambassador Hotel in Los Angeles. After leaving the stage and walking into the kitchen area of the hotel, Kennedy was shot by Sirhan Sirhan, a 24-year-old Jordanian living in Los Angeles. The motive for the shooting was apparently anger at several pro-Israeli speeches Kennedy had made during the campaign.

JUNE 6, VIETNAM

Dear Carol,

I was up to my ears with frustrations which stem from the hospital here. Honey, I know I could do nothing, say nothing, and just not care and nobody would ever care. However, I have never done anything half way intentionally and I don't want to start now.

I want to be able to say I did the best I could. So anyway last night I went up to that bar and got completely plastered. I was so sick I didn't even go to work in the morning. I did go this afternoon, however. Even though I got sick, I feel better after just completely letting go. I think it may have been worth it. In my situation last night, I didn't manage to get any letters off.

Today we heard the news of Robert Kennedy which is so very, very sad for so many reasons. I am afraid that this sort of thing is becoming a trend in our country and this is frightening. What can you say or do? I wish there was a way to undo it all.

KENNEDY IS DEAD; VICTIM OF ASSASSIN

June 6, Los Angeles, CA: Robert Kennedy died at age 42 in the early morning.

PRESIDENT JOHNSON ASKS CONGRESS FOR STRONG GUN CONTROL MEASURES

June 6, Washington, DC: President Johnson reacted to the death of Senator Robert F. Kennedy today by imploring Congress and the 50 Governors not to settle for "halfway" measures of gun control.

KENNEDY'S BODY FLOWN INTO NY CITY

June 7, New York City, NY: The body of Senator Robert Francis Kennedy returned to NY City, a home to the Senator for the last five years. His body will ultimately find rest with an Arlington burial.

ROBERT KENNEDY FUNERAL TODAY

June 8, New York, NY: Robert Kennedy's funeral was held at St. Patrick's Cathedral in New York. Senator Edward Kennedy delivered the eulogy. After the service, the body and 700 guests departed on a special train for the burial at Arlington National Cemetery in Virginia.

LETTERS HOME FROM VIETNAM   **CURRENT EVENTS**

JUNE 10, VIETNAM

Dear Carol,

The war is raging at a fantastic pace now and Honey, it is vicious. I see the results of it every day and we are still working ourselves into exhaustion. Believe me even the emergency room [in Birmingham, Alabama] never even approached this. Let me assure you, however, we are quite safe here, so don't worry.

Today I received a letter from Grandad, which was written by Uncle Nathan. This I appreciated very much.

HUMPHREY APPEARS TO BE ASSURED OF NOMINATION BY KENNEDY'S DELEGATE VOTES

June 10, Washington, DC: The nomination of Vice President Hubert Humphrey to be the Democratic presidential candidate moved closer to reality because Humphrey stands to inherit such a large share of the national convention delegates left unattached by the death of Senator Robert F. Kennedy.

HIGH COURT BACKS RIGHTS OF POLICE TO STOP AND FRISK

June 10, Washington, DC: The Supreme Court upheld the authority of policemen to stop suspicious-looking persons and frisk them for weapons when that is reasonably necessary for the safety of policemen and others.

JUNE 14, VIETNAM

Dear Carol,

We are in the beginning stages of what I fear is a hepatitis epidemic, Mac and I are busily looking for carriers and passing out gamma globulin. We are trying to inoculate a group of about 400 people, and believe me this is a job. I had my Gamma Globulin this a.m. and I can hardly sit down.

TIME MAGAZINE COVER

June 14, New York, NY: The Time magazine cover featured a drawing of the late Robert Kennedy.

LETTERS HOME FROM VIETNAM   **CURRENT EVENTS**

JUNE 15, VIETNAM

Dear Carol,
Today I received two letters and a tape from you, Darling.
They were just what the doctor ordered. We have been up
to our ears in work and as I lay here tonight, I don't think
I have ever been so absolutely exhausted. The civilian
casualties are so many and so bad that it just wears you
down day after day after day. All this plus the hepatitis
epidemic we are trying to stop has left me completely
exhausted.

JUNE 18, VIETNAM

Dear Carol,
Today was one hell of a busy day. I did a laparotomy, a
couple of amputations and a couple of delayed closures.
The surgeons can have it. I miss O.B. Not much other
news. Right now I am taking steroids and antihistamines to
combat an urticarial rash I managed to pick up somewhere.

JUNE 19, VIETNAM

Dear Carol,
Well you really wouldn't believe today. I did 5 major op
cases. Honey, there can't be many more people to
operate on.

KENNEDY FAMILY THANKS NATION FOR PROVIDING THEM WITH "STRENGTH AND HOPE"

June 15, Hyannis Port, MA:
From their home in Hyannis Port, Massachusetts, the brother and mother of Senator Robert F. Kennedy thanked the nation for its sympathy and pledged to "carry on the principles for which Bobby stood."

HIGH COURT RULES 1866 "RACIAL" HOUSING LAW UNCONSTITUTIONAL

June 18, Washington, DC: The Supreme Court turned an almost forgotten civil rights law of 1866 into a sweeping fair housing statute in a 7-to-2 ruling that prohibits racial discrimination in all sales and rentals of property.

CRIME CONTROL AND SAFE STREETS ACT

June 19, Washington, DC: The Omnibus Crime Control and Safe Streets Act of 1968 was passed by Congress and signed into law by President Lyndon B. Johnson. It established the Law Enforcement Assistance Administration, setting rules to obtain wiretap orders after November 22, 1963, when evidence in the assassination of President John F. Kennedy increased public alertness to the relative lack of control over the sale and possession of guns in the United States.

LETTERS HOME FROM VIETNAM	CURRENT EVENTS

JUNE 20, VIETNAM

Dear Carol,
Today was another one of those unbelievable days. As usual I am exhausted and as usual, I am in bed as I write this letter to you.

JUNE 21, VIETNAM

Dear Carol,
Today was still another hectic and frustrating day and I am glad it is over with. The only thing that went right today was my tennis game. I completely screwed up a man's foot today and the "local MDs" are still driving me crazy. But I just decided to say the hell with them. Ha!

JUNE 22, VIETNAM

Dear Carol,
Today I received the anatomy book you sent but I still have not received the OB. There is really nothing new here. The war is still raging and the casualties are pouring in. I too live for the day I will be home for good Darling.

PROTESTERS CALL FOR SHARING OF NATION'S AFFLUENCE BY ALL

June 19, Washington, DC: More than 50,000 orderly Americans marched to emphasize their demand for a just share of affluence and dignity for Negroes, Spanish-speaking minorities, American Indians, and poor whites.

HOUSE PASSES BILL TO INCREASE INCOME TAXES

June 20, Washington, DC: After more than 10 months of controversy and delay, the House approved a tax increase bill today by 268 to 150. It will go to the Senate on June 21st where it is expected to pass.

LIFE MAGAZINE COVERS KENNEDY

June 21, New York, NY: The latest issue of Life magazine featured "King and Kennedy Assassins Ray and Sirhan Psycho-biology of Violence."

HUMPHREY GAINS 14 IN MINNESOTA IN DELEGATE TEST

June 22, St. Paul, MN: Vice President Humphrey captured 14 more primary delegate votes from his home state.

LETTERS HOME FROM VIETNAM   **CURRENT EVENTS**

JUNE 23, VIETNAM

Dear Carol,
The war is raging at an alarming rate. Some of our people
are right now in heavy contact with a V.C. Battalion in
Vinh Binh subsection of Vinh Long[1] Province. I can feel the
air strikes 40 miles away. Tomorrow will be a busy day for
me. I don't care how many V.C. are injured, there will be
more civilian injuries.

JUNE 25, VIETNAM

Dear Carol,
Things are pretty rough over here now, especially up in
Saigon. I am debating whether to go up there now or not to
forecast. Don't worry, I will not go up there with things as
hot as they are now.

MCCARTHY SUPPORTERS STORM OUT OF CONNECTICUT STATE CONVENTION

June 22, Hartford, CT: More than 200 delegates supporting Senator Eugene J. McCarthy for president stormed out of the Connecticut Democratic state convention to protest what they considered unfair treatment by John M. Bailey's state party organization.

RESURRECTION CITY CLOSED DOWN BY FORCE

June 23, Washington, DC: A shanty town called Resurrection City, set up on Washington's National Mall, was closed down by tear gas. It was established by the Southern Christian Leadership Conference as part of the Poor People's Campaign to open the eyes of people to the conditions of poverty through this illustrative slum.

PEACE CORPS VOLUNTEERS DROP

June 23, Washington, DC: Some of the gleam is off the Peace Corps, but nobody in authority is ready to say why or even concede that it is so. Nevertheless, the number of volunteers overseas and of qualified applicants has been declining, and for the second consecutive year the corps proposes to spend more for

---

[1] Vinh Binh was a province in the Mekong Delta region of southern Vietnam. It was merged in the 1976 to Cuu Long and in 1992 re-spilt as Tra Vinh Province.

LETTERS HOME FROM VIETNAM

CURRENT EVENTS

JUNE 26, VIETNAM

Dear Carol,

I am still busy here and things are going to get a lot worse before they get better. Mac is going on R&R July 13 for 10 days. Then, in the middle of August, he is going back to the U.S. for a 30-day leave. This is because he is extending over here for 6 months. By the way he will call you when he goes back to the U.S. Well that's about it for now Darling.

HOUSE PANEL COOL TO PRESIDENT'S CALL FOR STIFF GUN LAW

June 25, Washington, DC: The Administration appeared today to have complicated its chances of pushing gun control legislation through the House by broadening its proposals to include registration and licensing controls.

ABE FORTAS NAMED

June 26, Washington, DC: President Johnson announced that he had named Associate Justice Abe Fortas to succeed Chief Justice Earl Warren.

RAMSEY CLARK URGES SENATORS TO SUPPORT THE REGISTRATION OF FIREARMS

June 26, Washington, DC: Attorney General Ramsey Clark told a Senate subcommittee today that Congress would be failing in its responsibility to check crime if it did not include registration and licensing of firearms in a gun control bill.

July 1968

JULY 1, VIETNAM

Dear Carol,

Today I had a very depressing day as I had the unpleasant job of doing 4 amputations. On one little 7-year-old boy, I had to do 2 above the knee amputations. This gave me a very empty feeling and I almost cried. I know they had to be done, but this little boy never did anything to anybody. What could a 7-year-old boy do? Well, Darling, soon this nightmare will all be over. When it is, I hope I can push it into the back of my mind and never think about it again.

JULY 2, VIETNAM

Dear Carol,

Every day here is about the same. I see an endless amount of blood, guts, gore and death. I have never seen so much death in my life. I see more people die in 2 weeks than I saw during my entire medical school and internship period. The absolute butchery of human beings at times becomes overwhelming.

UAW SEPARATES

July 1, Detroit MI: The United Auto Workers formally separated from the AFL-CIO.

NEW STUDY SHOWS SMOKING PERILS

July 1, Washington, DC: The average young man who is a heavy cigarette smoker can expect to have his life shortened by eight years if he continues the habit, the Public Health Service reported today.

CARDINAL COOKE APPOINTS NEGRO PASTOR

July 2, New York, NY: Archbishop Terence J. Cooke announced that he had named the Archdiocese of New York's first Negro pastor, at the same time appointing him as vicariate delegate for Harlem.

| LETTERS HOME FROM VIETNAM | CURRENT EVENTS |

JULY 3, VIETNAM

Dear Carol,

I wish there was something new to tell you about, but every day is the same; surgery, surgery, and more surgery. Today we played 3 games of tennis and then got completely wiped out by the monsoon rains. Every day we are getting closer to Hawaii and I just can't wait. My every thought every day is getting back to you.

JULY 4, VIETNAM

Dear Carol,

Today is July 4th and would you believe that I did 2 cases this a.m. and that I am actually caught up! I did absolutely nothing this afternoon and I enjoyed every minute of it. It is now 5:00 p.m. and I am already home from work. How about that!

JULY 5, VIETNAM

Dear Carol,

Today I repaired a cut brachial artery [the major blood vessel of the upper arm]. This is my 2nd such repair this week. These cases are generally rewarding. That's it for now.

CHURCH GROUPS TO BUY FROM BIAS-FREE UNIT

July 3, Long Island, NY: Seventeen Protestant, Roman Catholic, and Jewish groups from the Long Island area said that they would try to channel their millions of dollars in purchasing and building funds only to companies and unions that give equal employment opportunities to minority groups.

GUNMAN TERRORIZES CENTRAL PARK

July 4, New York, NY: A man who lived in an apartment hung with pictures of Nazi leaders shot to death a young woman, critically wounded an elderly man, and wounded two patrolmen in a murderous foray in Central Park before being killed by policemen.

WILKINS, IN TALK TO CORE, SEEKS TO CLOSE NEGRO RIFT

July 5, Columbus, OH: Roy Wilkins, a moderate among civil rights leaders, joined with leaders of the militant Congress of Racial Equality in urging cooperative efforts to benefit Negroes. Mr. Wilkins called such unity "a necessity if black people are going to successfully attack the problems that beset them."

JULY 15, VIETNAM

Dear Carol,

Things are beginning to quiet down a little but everyone is tense in anticipation of the big offensive we are supposed to be getting in July. Everyone is trigger happy and I just know that someone is going to get shot accidentally. I have been able to play quite a bit of tennis lately. Actually, if Mac were here, I wouldn't be very busy at all. However, the double load keeps me busy.

JULY 16, VIETNAM

Dear Carol,

After a few days of relative quiet things perked up a bit last night as the town got hit pretty hard with mortars. Actually I slept through all of that but I did find a hospital full of wounded patients this a.m. Mac is still on R&R so you can see how busy I must be now.

JULY 18, VIETNAM

Dear Carol,

Things have stepped up again here. The casualties are coming in again. I bet that I have already done 250–300 major cases since I have been here, and it doesn't look like things are going to change. Well that's it for now. Remember that I love you very much.

SOME NYC FIREMEN CARRYING BLACKJACKS ON SLUM CALLS

July 15, New York, NY: Some firemen here have begun arming themselves with blackjacks when they respond to alarms in slums where youths have attacked them. Most of the assaults have been with rocks, bricks, and bottles thrown from roofs or alleys, but recently there have been scattered attacks at close range by youths who have beaten the firemen with sticks or threatened them with knives.

SENATE HEARS TESTIMONY ON FORTAS NOMINATION

July 16, Washington, DC: Testimony was heard before the Senate Judiciary Committee regarding the nomination of Abe Fortas to be chief justice of the United States.

EISENHOWER BACKS NIXON FOR THE PRESIDENCY

July 18, Washington, DC: Former president Dwight D. Eisenhower endorsed Richard M. Nixon for the Republican presidential nomination. The 77-year-old general said that Nixon was experienced and could be decisive. He added that he was fully equipped to deal with the problems facing the nation.

LETTERS HOME FROM VIETNAM

CURRENT EVENTS

JULY 22, VIETNAM

Dear Carol,

I have overcome my depression for the time being and hope you are feeling better. I guess that's what a tour in Vietnam is a series of depression until one happy day when all of a sudden it is all over. We are getting there. . . . I am enclosing a picture that one of my medics took. I don't know what I was doing then, and I probably didn't know at the time either.

The last couple of days have been relatively quiet, which has allowed me to take it easy. Things run in cycles here and I am sure that in a few days I will be snowed under again. I am thankful for the rest however. It has been a long time since I have had just one case to do all day. How about that!

By the way, this looks like a fairly nice operating room to be found in Vietnam. Actually the OR is very nice, but the rest of the hospital isn't. I will send you some pictures of it if the camera ever gets here. Please be sure to show this picture to Mother and Dad as they certainly would like to see it.

RAY'S TRIAL SET FOR NOVEMBER 12 AFTER HE PLEADS NOT GUILTY

July 22, Memphis, TN: James Earl Ray pleaded not guilty in Memphis, Tennessee, to a charge that he murdered the Rev. Dr. Martin Luther King Jr. last April 4. His trial was set to begin November 12. The date was picked to avoid the presidential election held the first week of November.

GOVERNORS UNANIMOUSLY PRAISE JOHNSON

July 22, Cincinnati, OH: The nation's governors adopted unanimously today a resolution praising President Johnson for "his long and devoted public service," a move designed to lure him into a personal appearance in Cincinnati for tomorrow night.

LETTERS HOME FROM VIETNAM   **CURRENT EVENTS**

JULY 24, VIETNAM

Dear Carol,

Things have continued to be quiet around here. I did 2 majors this a.m. and I did absolutely nothing this afternoon. The tension is growing and growing in expectation of that new offensive. I can honestly say that I think that these people are ready for an attack of any kind. When and if this offensive comes, it certainly won't be a surprise to anyone.

JULY 25, VIETNAM

Dear Carol,

Today business started picking up again as I knew it would. I did not receive any mail today, except a letter from Uncle Nathan. I'm sure tomorrow I'll get a letter from you. I have been keeping up with the presidential campaign quite faithfully through the newspaper and through Times and New Yorker magazines. The death of Robert Kennedy certainly put a damper on what started out to be a very energetic campaign. I don't think there is much doubt that all this campaigning will lead to a final decision between Humphrey and Nixon. I would be highly surprised to see one of the "Peace Candidates," McCarthy or Rockefeller slip into their party nomination. At any rate, I am supporting Nixon. I feel that he is the only man who can get us out of Vietnam in an honorable way. I want to get out of here but I'd like to do it with some sort of victory. I think Nixon can come closest to accomplishing this. What I want to know is, are you going to join me in supporting Nixon or are we going to cancel each other's vote? If you say that you are going to vote for Wallace, I will wring your neck. Certainly my wife wouldn't do that. Well Darling, that's about it for now.

ARLO GUTHRIE PERFORMS

July 24, Newport, RI: At the Newport (Rhode Island) Folk Festival, singer Arlo Guthrie performed his 20-minute ballad, "Alice's Restaurant," to rave reviews.

CLEVELAND MAYOR SENDS GUARD BACK TO PATROL SLUMS

July 25, Cleveland, OH: Mayor Carl B. Stokes ordered the police and Ohio National Guardsmen to return to the East Side. He abandoned the All-Negro Citizens' Patrols he had established in the area after an outbreak of looting. It was a request made by the community.

PERCY ENDORSES ROCKEFELLER BID FOR PRESIDENCY

July 25, Washington, DC: Senator Charles H. Percy of Illinois endorsed Governor Rockefeller of New York for the Republican nomination for President today.

JULY 28, VIETNAM

Dear Carol,

We are in the middle of a physician's disagreement here, as Fred Seaman and I have a difference in opinion with Mac. Mac feels that we should take night calls on these patients at the hospital. Fred and I feel that it is an unnecessary risk. They have their own physicians there who even live at the hospital. I think we do enough work during the day.

How is school? I hope you are getting ready for your finals. I have been taking pictures right and left.

WALLACE GAINS SIGNATURES FOR RHODE ISLAND PRIMARY BID AMIDST JEERS FROM SOME IN THE CROWD

July 26, Providence, RI: Gov. George Wallace garnered more than twice the 500 signatures needed to be eligible to run in the Rhode Island presidential primary as an independent. When a large crowd of Negroes and white supporters for their cause began to jeer during his speech, he remarked: "These are the folks our country is getting sick and tired of. You'de better have your time now, because after November, I tell you, you are through."

GOP FACES FIGHT OVER SENATOR DIRKSEN'S IDEA ON VIETNAM PARTY PLANK

July 28, Washington, DC: The Senate Republican leader, Everett McKinley Dirksen, encountered possible dissension in conservative Republican ranks over his intention not to make the Vietnam War a partisan issue in the Republican platform.

JULY 30, VIETNAM

Dear Carol,

I just read a long article in the New Yorker about Garrison[2] in New Orleans. The article did two things; it confused the hell out of me and it made me really miss New Orleans.

JULY 31, VIETNAM

Dear Carol,

All here has been very quiet as far as the hospital is concerned, but last night the V.C. really drove the rockets and mortars into the airfield. Fortunately, no one was hurt. I climbed down from the ceiling at about 3:00 a.m. and went back to sleep. Those damn things are loud as hell. Last night I sent 3 rolls of film to San Francisco to be developed.

$25.4 BILLION DEFICIT IS LARGEST

July 30, Washington, DC: The Treasury and the Budget Bureau reported that the final budget results for the fiscal year 1968, ended a month ago, showed a deficit of $25.4 billion, the largest since World War II.

PRESIDENT JOHNSON ASSAILS BETHLEHEM STEEL FOR 5 PERCENT RISE

July 31, Washington, DC: President Johnson said that the 5 percent across-the-board steel price increase announced by the Bethlehem Steel Corporation would, if followed by the rest of the industry, have "dire economic consequences for our nation."

---

[2]James Carothers "Jim" Garrison was the district attorney of Orleans Parish, Louisiana, from 1962 to 1973. A member of the Democratic Party, he is best known for his investigations into the assassination of President John F. Kennedy. He was played by Kevin Costner in Oliver Stone's JFK.

August 1968

AUGUST 2, VIETNAM

Dear Carol,
I have been reading my Times Magazine rather faithfully.
I have never been so well up on current events. I read my
OB-GYN, pretty much at my leisure. I have been keeping up
with the campaign, the controversy with the Supreme Court,
the unrest in Central Europe and of course, the fiasco here in
Vietnam.

AUGUST 4, VIETNAM

Dear Carol,
I am glad to hear that you are planning to join me in voting
for Nixon. I have confidence that he will get us out of here
in an honorable way. I will have to disagree with you on
George Wallace, as I don't think he has even a fraction of
what it takes to be a president. Our country is faced with
so many dangers now from within and from without and
I don't think that George Wallace has the experience or the
judgment to help us. As a matter of fact, I think he would be
the initiating factor in the development of a frank civil war
at home.

ACCUSED ASSASSIN OF RFK PLEADS NOT GUILTY

August 2, Los Angeles, CA:
Sirhan B. Sirhan pleaded not guilty to a charge of first-degree murder in the fatal June 5 shooting of 42-year-old Senator Robert F. Kennedy. The trial was set for November 1st.

NIXON'S TWO RIVALS STRIVING TO BLOCK HIM ON FIRST VOTE

August 4, Albany, NY: Nelson Rockefeller of New York and Ronald Reagan of California take personal charge of their parallel campaigns to deny first-ballot nomination to Richard M. Nixon at the Republican National Convention.

AUGUST 8, VIETNAM

Dear Carol,

Today we heard that Nixon officially got the nomination and I am glad that as a family we can cast 2 votes for him. It is quite disconcerting, however, to think that regardless of who we vote for and regardless of who wins, the Alabama popular vote, the electoral vote will be literally wasted on George Wallace. I am really afraid that he could take just enough Republican votes out of the South to put Humphrey into office. Tomorrow is a big day for me as I become a neurosurgeon. We are starting to do a little intracranial work. Some live, some die. Well Darling, that's about it for now. PS—Honey, I need some batteries for my tape recorder. That's why the tapes sound so funny. OK?

AUGUST 15, VIETNAM

Dear Carol,

It is Thursday afternoon and I am enjoying an afternoon off because of a Vietnamese holiday. I have been playing tennis all afternoon and now I am writing a few letters before supper. Mac is gone now and I am already feeling the increased pressure. I am enclosing some pictures which were taken at the hospital. This will give you a better idea of why this place can get so terribly depressing at times.

NIXON WINS NOMINATION

August 8, Miami, FL: At their party convention in Miami Beach, the Republicans nominated Richard Milhouse Nixon to be their presidential candidate. His running mate will be Spiro Agnew of Maryland. Challengers to Nixon were Nelson Rockefeller of New York and Ronald Reagan of California.

NIXON PLEDGES END TO WAR; CALLS FOR A WAR ON CRIME

August 8, Miami, FL: Richard M. Nixon called for "new leadership" to restore the nation's prestige abroad and heal its wounds at home. He declared that "the long, dark night for America is about to end."Reminisent of the words from a Martin L. King speech, he added: "The time for us has come to leave the valley of despair and climb the mountain so that we may see the glory of a new day for America, a new dawn for peace and freedom to the world."

NARCOTICS DEATHS ON INCREASE IN NYC

August 15, New York, NY: Diseases related to narcotics addiction have been reported to cause more deaths among New Yorkers 15 to 35 years old than murder, suicide, accidents, or natural causes, according to a report issued by the city's medical examiner, Dr. Milton Helpern.

LETTERS HOME FROM VIETNAM   **CURRENT EVENTS**

AUGUST 16, VIETNAM

Dear Carol,

Hi Darling . . . All here is about the same. With Mac gone, my workload has increased somewhat but really nothing too dreadful. I am still playing tennis every day and this is still a great outlet. Unfortunately, my tennis partner, Ray Brewer, is leaving September 2nd. Ray is the ophthalmologist I was telling you about. Mac will be calling you in a few days. I would be careful not to discuss politics with him as we disagree somewhat on how things should be done over here. Mac is a real nice guy however and he is a real friend. In 5 months he has operated on me twice; once on my foot and once on my abdomen.

Up until now I have been the only Jewish boy in the entire province. Now we have a new Army Major, Murray Schooner, who is also Jewish. He is a real nice guy and it is great having him around although I really don't know him too well. Well Darling, that's about it for now. Tell Mac hello for me when he calls.

STAR OF THE GOP CAMPAIGN COACHES HIS STAND

August 16, California: Richard M. Nixon, who spent all week on the telephone with luminaries from the left wing of his party, conferred face-to-face with the hero of its right: Governor Ronald Reagan of California.

EISENHOWER SUFFERS ANOTHER HEART ATTACK

August 16, Washington, DC: Former President Dwight D. Eisenhower suffered another serious heart attack and it was his second in two weeks. Physicians at Walter Reed Army Medical Center said the 77-year old General was in stable condition.

MCCARTHY PICKS UP STATE DELEGATES

August 16, Syracuse, NY: Supporters of Senator Eugene J. McCarthy and Negroes and Puerto Ricans gained additional representation on the Democratic delegation to the National Convention at a quiet meeting of the Democratic State Committee here today.

LETTERS HOME FROM VIETNAM   **CURRENT EVENTS**

AUGUST 17, VIETNAM

Dear Carol,

Well today marks the end of 5 months and now we are into our 6th month. I'll be seeing you in about 12 weeks. How does that sound? Today things were back to their old pace, as I spent almost the entire day in the operating room. I never even made it to lunch and I didn't get home from the hospital until late. When Mac calls tell him we are managing OK, but we are busy as hell.

AUGUST 19, VIETNAM

Dear Carol,

Here we are into 6th month. Not too much longer before R&R. Boy, I can't wait. Everyone here is very nervously awaiting the August offensive we are supposed to have. This is the "3rd offensive" you hear so much about. Waiting can really get on one's nerves. I do take great comfort in the fact we have over twice as many Americans in this area as they had during Tet.

I'm still pretty busy at the hospital with Mac gone, but somehow I am managing OK. I can only do so much in one day, and when the day is over, I just stop.

GOVERNOR MADDOX SEEKS DEMOCRATIC PRESIDENTIAL NOMINATION

August 17, Atlanta, GA: Governor Lester G. Maddox of Georgia, invoking God and talking enthusiastically of miracles, announced that he would seek the Democratic presidential nomination to represent the "conservative element of American society."

DEMOCRATS CLASH OVER CONVENTION CREDENTIALS

August 19, Chicago, IL: Delegates from Mississippi were challenged as to whether they included Negro participation. The state Democrats argued they had made remarkable progress toward inclusion.

FORMER PRESIDENT EISENHOWER RESTS AS SPASMS DECREASE

August 19, Washington, DC: Former President Dwight D. Eisenhower fought for his life against mounting odds tonight. His doctors described his condition as "critical." Doctors have ruled out a heart transplant due to the General's age and other factors.

LETTERS HOME FROM VIETNAM

CURRENT EVENTS

AUGUST 22, VIETNAM

Dear Carol,

Things have really been busy as today was another one of those dreadfully busy days. As you are probably reading in the paper we are getting plenty of action in this area. The civilian casualties are more numerous now that I have seen since I have been here. I just do as much as I can in a day and what I can't do just has to wait. Would you believe that we have not been able to play tennis for 2 days!

AUGUST 23, VIETNAM

Dear Carol,

I fell asleep reading last night. I just wanted to get this note to you to tell you that I love you very much. Yesterday was one of the bloodiest days I have seen at this hospital. I spent the whole day in the operating room and I was absolutely exhausted last night. I think I must have fallen asleep at 9:00 p.m. or something.

AUGUST 25, VIETNAM

Dear Carol,

We are still busy as hell at the hospital and the surgery schedule every day is almost unbelievable. I am doing 4–5 cases each day and I would do more but time just doesn't allow it. Every day I just wish I knew more so I could provide more and better medical care to these people. I assure you, however, I will continue to do the absolute best I can. I just hope that this will be enough more often than not.

KENNEDY ATTACKS VIETNAM POLICY

August 22, Chicago, IL: Exploring the tension in the Democrat Party, Senator Edward M. Kennedy announced that he was picking up the fallen standard of his brothers and called for the removal of "our men and our future" from the "bottomless pit" of Vietnam.

TEXANS PROPOSE BACKING JOHNSON FOR PARTY NOMINATION

August 23, Chicago, IL: A proposal to re-nominate President Johnson at the Democratic National Convention next week was put forward by a rebellious Texas delegation. Governor Connally reported growing sentiment in the state for Johnson.

THE DEMOCRATIC PARTY AND TROOPS CONVERGE ON CHICAGO FOR THE CONVENTION

August 25, Chicago, IL: As the Democrats gathered there for the national convention in Chicago, tensions rose in the streets and protesters were met by armed troops.

LETTERS HOME FROM VIETNAM   **CURRENT EVENTS**

AUGUST 26, VIETNAM

Dear Carol,

I am glad that Mac called and that you had a nice conversation with him. He really is a nice guy and as I have said many times, I have a lot of respect for him. I also wish that he were back here now. I walked into the hospital this morning and found 41 new war casualties. Where in the hell do you start? I did 5 major cases, Fred Seaman did 2 and we still have many left. This was all the result of a mortar attack last night on the town and in the sub-sectors. Would you believe that I did a saphenous vein graft[3] to repair a cut axillary artery.[4] I don't know if it will work, but I tried. Only time will tell.

YIPPIE PRESENCE AT CONVENTION

August 26, Chicago, IL: The Yippie movement was at the center of action during the Chicago Democratic National Convention, hosting a Festival of Life in contrast to what they term the convention's Festival of Death.

MAYOR DALEY OPENS DEMOCRATIC CONVENTION

August 26, Chicago, IL: Mayor Richard Daley opened the Democratic National Convention in Chicago. While the convention moved haltingly toward nominating Hubert Humphrey for president, the city's police attempted to enforce an 11 o'clock curfew. Demonstrations were widespread, but generally peaceful. The next two days, however, brought increasing tension and violence to the situation.

---

[3] The saphenous vein, also called long saphenous vein, is the large (subcutaneous) superficial vein of the leg and thigh (see "Great Saphenous Vein," InnerBody, www.innerbody.com/image_cardov/card29-new.html)

[4] The axillary artery is a large blood vessel that conveys oxygenated blood to the thorax (see "Axillary Artery," InnerBody, www.inner-body.com/image_cardov/card35-new.html)

| LETTERS HOME FROM VIETNAM | CURRENT EVENTS |

AUGUST 27, VIETNAM

Dear Carol,

Last night the V.C. hit the airfield with the heaviest mortar and ground attack I have seen since I have been here. Actually I sat by my window and watched every single bit of it, the V.C. mortars and the allied reactionary helicopter attacks. However, I am OK, so don't worry about me. As I am sure you can imagine, this offensive has brought with it a fantastic number of civilian casualties. Again today, I spent the entire day in the operating room. I did 5 major cases and I never set foot outside the door until it was time to go home this evening. However, let me emphasize that I am OK. Today I received no mail because the attack on the airfield injured 3 of the 4 mail clerks.

AUGUST 28, VIETNAM

Dear Carol,

Today was another dreadful day and again I spent the entire day in the operating room. Needless to say I am tired as hell. Last night the V.C. hit the town again with a mortar attack, but I slept through it all. The patients were stacked up like sardines when I got to the hospital. Mac has been gone 2 weeks and I must confess I am ready for him to come back. I am tired as hell. I still did not receive any mail from you today although I did receive a tape from Mother. As I said before, with this new offensive everything is all screwed up. I hope some of the mail is getting through to you.

DEMOCRATIC CANDIDATES MEET FACE-TO-FACE

August 27, Chicago, IL: The three leading candidates for the Democratic presidential nomination met face-to-face in Chicago, before the California convention delegation, in the first such encounter of the campaign.

DEMOCRATIC CONVENTION BREAKS UP IN ANGER

August 28, Chicago, IL: The Democratic National Convention broke up in anger and confusion early in the morning, just a few minutes after the start of the long-awaited debate on the Vietnam plank of the 1968 platform.

CHICAGO POLICE GO AFTER PROTESTORS

August 28, Chicago, IL: Chicago police took action against crowds of demonstrators without provocation. The police beat some marchers unconscious, sent at least 100 to emergency rooms, and arrested 175. Mayor Daley explained, "The policeman isn't there to create disorder, the policeman is there to preserve disorder."

AUGUST 29, VIETNAM

Dear Carol,

Today things slowed down a little. I think I have finally caught up with all my surgery, now I have a lot of elective stuff to take care of. The offensive has been slowing down a little here, although our intelligence people say that there will be one more big push. I hope I can get all of my elective stuff out of the way before the next push. Honey, the other night while the airfield was under V.C. mortar and ground attack, I sat here at my window and recorded some of the actual sounds of that battle and I narrated a little of it to you. However, I have delayed in sending it to you because I'm afraid it might scare you. . . . I feel quite safe here and there really isn't too much to worry about. If you would be interested in that tape I will send it to you, but I don't want to send it if you think it might scare you.

HUMPHREY NOMINATED ON THE FIRST BALLOT AFTER HIS PLANK ON VIETNAM IS APPROVED

August 29, Chicago, IL: While a pitched battle between the police and thousands of young antiwar demonstrators raged in the streets of Chicago, the Democratic National Convention nominated Hubert H. Humphrey for president, on a platform reflecting his and President Johnson's views on the war in Vietnam.

THOUSANDS MARCH AT CONVENTION

August 29, Chicago, IL: More than 150 people, including nine convention delegates, were arrested last night after National Guardsmen halted 3,000 persons marching toward the International Amphitheatre.

LETTERS HOME FROM VIETNAM	CURRENT EVENTS

AUGUST 30, VIETNAM

Dear Carol,

I will be brief tonight as I am very, very tired. Today was hell and again I spent all day in the operating room and I just wonder how many more people are going to be injured here. I see this every day and I still can't believe it. Would you believe that I spent all day in a lady's brain? One more day and I will get a little rest.

AUGUST 31, VIETNAM

Dear Carol,

Finally, this busy week has come to an end and I am now catching my breath here on Saturday evening. I can't remember ever having been so tired, mentally and physically. Tomorrow is Sunday and I'm really looking forward to the rest. I was able to play tennis today and I plan to play again in the morning.

Ray Brewer, the ophthalmologist I have referred to several times, is leaving in the next couple of days and I really hate to see him go. I have enjoyed his being here and I have enjoyed playing tennis with him. One can certainly make some good friends over here, so that's one thing Vietnam is good for.

Well it looks like it will be Nixon vs. HHH just as everyone expected. I sure hope Nixon can win this thing. I hate to think that HHH might be president of the U.S.

HUMPHREY TAKES COMMAND OF THE PARTY

August 30, Washington, DC: Hubert H. Humphrey moved to take personal control of the Democratic Party for his presidential campaign and establish his independence as a candidate.

OUTDOOR ROCK FESTIVAL

August 30, Washington: The Sky River Rock Festival and Lighter Than Air Fair opened a three-day run in a pasture near Sultan in Snohomish County, located in Washington State. This is one of America's first multiday, outdoor rock concerts. Among the bands and performers playing were Santana and the Grateful Dead.

THE NATIONAL GUARD LEAVES CHICAGO AS POLICE END 12-HOUR TOURS

August 31, Chicago, IL: Illinois National Guardsmen, who took up positions in Chicago for a week to protect the Democratic National Convention, left their armories and headed for home. The city was unbelievably peaceful.

September 1968

SEPTEMBER 1, VIETNAM

Dear Carol,

This afternoon we are having a going away party for Ray who is leaving in the a.m. The boys managed to get a bunch of steaks and hamburger at the airfield and we are going to grill them at the nurses' house. We have two U.S. AID nurses on our team and they have a house of their own a few blocks down the street.

Not much news here today as Sunday is just a day of tennis and rest and that's exactly what I'm doing today. We are expecting another V.C. push and our intelligence sources predict tomorrow night, but our intelligence people are wrong more often than they are right.

SEPTEMBER 3, VIETNAM

Dear Carol,

Well enough for finances. Today was another awful day as I guess they all will be until Mac returns. Surgery, surgery, surgery all day, every day. You know it can really get old.

HUMPHREY KICKS OFF CAMPAIGN

September 1, New York, NY: Democratic nominee Hubert Humphrey kicked off his presidential campaign at New York City's Labor Day parade.

CLEVELAND SEEKS ANSWERS TO RACIAL UNREST IN CITY

September 2, Cleveland, OH: Mayor Carl B. Stokes wanted answers when he said: "There is something wrong with our society." He explained that: "Many of us have known this for a long while and have searched for the answers. But the answers have obviously not been found."He was looking back on a 4-day race battle in July when eleven men, nine Black and three white police officers, were killed.

MAYOR DALEY DEMANDS TELEVISION TIME TO DEFEND HIS POLICE DEPARTMENT

September 3, Chicago, IL: Mayor Richard J. Daley, angered at criticism of him and the Chicago police during the Democratic convention last week, demanded prime time from each of the major television networks to respond.

SEPTEMBER 6, VIETNAM

Dear Carol,

I have just finished up another one of those dreadful days where I was busy in the operating room all day. I haven't been able to play very much tennis with Mac gone. Not only that it has been raining like hell here. Not only that I am having a hard time finding someone to play with. Today the mailman didn't make it to Vinh Long. Actually I have received mail only once this week. The mail service is all screwed up in Saigon, but I really don't know why. Hopefully tomorrow they will get the lead out and get some mail down here.

PRESIDENT HINTS HE'LL PLAY DEFENSIVE CAMPAIGN ROLE

September 6, Washington, DC: President Johnson suggested that he and his cabinet members would be politically active this fall in defense of his administration, but he pledged himself to bipartisanship in keeping all candidates informed on foreign affairs.

CARRIER KENNEDY, COMMISSIONED, IS HANDED OVER TO NAVY BY CAROLINE

September 7, Newport News, VA: The aircraft carrier John F. Kennedy, a hulking gray ship more than 1,050 feet long and displacing some 88,000 tons, was ceremoniously handed over to the United States Navy today by young Caroline Kennedy. The vessel was named after her late father.

LETTERS HOME FROM VIETNAM

CURRENT EVENTS

SEPTEMBER 8, VIETNAM

Dear Carol,

Guess what? This new colonel here, who is really a No. 1 man, has put the cards on the table. He told us that if we are not satisfied with our counterpart, he will help us get rid of him. If we could get a Vietnamese physician or physicians here who could learn to take care of these people properly, then maybe we could prevent one American doctor somewhere from having to come over here or even maybe more. The purpose of our mission here in this hospital and in Vietnam in general is to eliminate the need for our presence here. When we can do this, no more Americans will have to make the same sacrifice that you and I are making and even more importantly, no more Americans will have to make that awful sacrifice that has already been made by over 26,000 Americans. I really don't know if we can ever eliminate the need for our presence here, but I know we can't if we continue to tolerate uncooperative counterparts. I feel that it is my duty as an American to do anything and everything I can to help bring this awful situation to a conclusion. When compared with the whole problem, this problem looks so small, but it is a lot of unsolved, small problems like this that has made the big picture look so absolutely hopeless.

This is not to ever mention my obligation as a physician to try to put an end to irresponsible and negligent medical practices. Every irresponsible act that I tolerate, I am in truth condoning and I am therefore as guilty as the man who has actually committed the irresponsible act. [By voting him out], the hurt that he feels will not be nearly so great and not nearly so lasting as the hurt felt by the millions of Americans who have lost loved ones in this country.

HUMPHREY DEFINES THE RACE FOR PRESIDENT

September 8, Washington, DC: Hubert H. Humphrey defined the 1968 campaign as a "referendum on human rights" and charged that Richard M. Nixon and George C. Wallace were in competition against him, trying to exploit "the fears and hates aroused by this issue."

NEWTON GUILTY OF MANSLAUGHTER

September 8, Oakland, CA: Huey P. Newton, the 26-year-old Black Panther leader, was convicted tonight of voluntary manslaughter in the killing of an Oakland policeman, John Frey. The verdict came after 8-days of jury deliberation in the eight-week trial. The verdict was considered a victory for the defense. If convicted of murder, Newton would have received the death penalty. He will now be sentenced from 2 to 15 years.

LETTERS HOME FROM VIETNAM	CURRENT EVENTS

SEPTEMBER 9, VIETNAM

Dear Carol,
It is very late and I am very tired so I will be brief. Not only that, but I have to get up at 6:00 a.m. to go check out a possible epidemic of smallpox. Boy, I hope that's not what these people have.

CHICAGO NEGROES LAUDED

September 9, Chicago, IL: The director of the National Advisory Commission on Civil Disorders criticized Mayor Richard J. Daley, the Chicago police, demonstrators, and the news media for their roles during the rioting while the Democratic National Convention met in Chicago.

SEPTEMBER 10, VIETNAM

Dear Carol,
This picture was taken this morning in a little Vietnamese village where I went to investigate what was thought to be an epidemic of smallpox. This little village was hit last night by the V.C. You can see in this picture where a mortar fragment went through this hut. There I am instructing a few Americans and their counterparts what to look for as far as smallpox in the civilian population is concerned. I'll tell you a secret; I was glad as hell to get out of that place. At any rate I don't think they have smallpox in that area at present. Please show this picture to Mother and Dad the next time you see them. I'm sending them one, but it isn't as good as this one.

That little trip killed my whole morning, so I had to operate until 8:00 p.m. tonight to catch up. Again I was glad to get out of that damn place, believe me. I had half of my team guarding the hospital while I operated. Boy, what a day!

NIXON PLEDGES MORE POWER TO RETURN TO THE STATES FOR HOME RULE

September 10, White Plains, NY: Richard M. Nixon opened his campaign for New York's 43 electoral votes tonight in the warm embrace of Governor Rockefeller and to the tumultuous cheers of a vocal Westchester County rally. He said Humphrey was running on the same policies as Johnson. Nixon wants power to be returned to the states.

LETTERS HOME FROM VIETNAM   **CURRENT EVENTS**

SEPTEMBER 11, VIETNAM

Dear Carol,

Today was another one of those dreadful days and again I spent almost the entire day in the operating room. Mac has been gone exactly one month today. He should be back in one week; at least I hope so. I'm tired as hell. I'm expecting Mac back on the 19th and I'm planning to go to Saigon on the 21st for services.[5] I am not going to Tokyo, at least not now.

SEPTEMBER 13, VIETNAM

Dear Carol,

Would you believe we finally had an easy day today. I only had 2 cases and I did them both this a.m. This afternoon I sat down all day and enjoyed the hell out of doing nothing. I did take my tape recorder to the hospital today and I recorded a little conversation with my little friend Loc. At 6 1/2 years of age, this little fellow is learning to speak English. I will complete this tape and send it to you. Today the mail man didn't make it to Vinh Long, so no mail. Hopefully I will get a double supply. At least I hope so.

Today another American Army battalion moved into the Vinh Long area. The more the merrier, as far as I'm concerned. However, I think it's becoming more evident the Vietnamese military cannot take care of this area without our help. This of course was the original plan, to let the Vietnamese take care of the Delta area themselves with Americans functioning only as advisors. You can see how much advising I'm doing.

[5] In September, the month of the Hebrew calendar. It is the religious services during the festival of Rosh Hashanah.

HUMPHREY SAYS NIXON IS A WIGGLER ON CRUCIAL ISSUES

September 11, Flint, MI: Vice President Humphrey attacked Richard M. Nixon as "a wiggler and a wobbler" on the most crucial issues. He said Nixon is the creator of doubts that he said were aggravating the international issues, such as the nonproliferation treaty, and domestic issues, such as law and order.

FORTAS REFUSES TO APPEAR AGAIN IN SENATE INQUIRY

September 13, Washington, DC: Associate Justice Abe Fortas refused to submit to further questioning by the Senate Judiciary Committee on his nomination to be chief justice of the United States. He gave no specific reason after the panel was told the justice got $15,000 in lecture fees.

ANTI-SEMITISM NOT FOUND IN FORTAS INQUIRY

September 13, Washington, DC: Senator Jacob K. Javits told the Senate that he had found "no hard evidence" that antiSemitism was behind the opposition to the confirmation of Associate Justice Abe Fortas as Chief Justice of the United States.

LETTERS HOME FROM VIETNAM

CURRENT EVENTS

SEPTEMBER 14, VIETNAM

Dear Carol,

Well here is another Saturday and a hard one it has been. But now it's over and tomorrow is Sunday and I'm so glad of it. Today I did 5 majors and as usual I am exhausted. I was just reviewing some statistics and I notice that I have done about 175 major cases since Mac has been gone. This is averaging better than 5 a day. I get tired just thinking about that. Well, at least I can rest tomorrow. I love those Sundays.

Not really much news. . . . I'm just working and sleeping and that's about it. It is a real problem finding someone to talk with around here. I just don't have anything in common with the military people. I get just as sick of hearing about war as they get hearing about medicine.

NIXON LEADS IN 30 STATES SEPTEMBER 14,

Washington, DC: If the presidential election were held now, Richard M. Nixon would win a sweeping Republican victory, a national political survey revealed. The survey was conducted by the New York Times.

NIXON PROPOSES RURAL AID TO ARREST MOVES TO CITIES

September 14, Des Moines, Iowa: Richard M. Nixon proposed today to help the American farmer in particular and the nation as a whole by arresting the migration from the countryside to the city. As he views the Johnson administration failures, he and his advisors believe that rural poverty must be reduced and the economic attractiveness of the rural America must be addressed.

LETTERS HOME FROM VIETNAM   **CURRENT EVENTS**

SEPTEMBER 15, VIETNAM

Dear Carol,

This morning I went down to make rounds as I usually do on Sunday. However, instead of leaving right after rounds, I found myself there, operating until 2:00 p.m. Today I had to operate on a child with a depressed skull fracture and an adult with a compound comminuted fracture of her femur. However, I was determined to play tennis and this I did this afternoon.

SEPTEMBER 16, VIETNAM

Dear Carol,

Today was as busy as all days have been around here. Today I spent all afternoon repairing a femoral artery that had been shot through and through. To make matters worse, I received a letter from Mac informing me that he would not be back until the 23rd. I was expecting him back on the 17th or 18th. Well there goes one trip to Saigon. I will be going up on October 1 however and this is when I will get in our R&R application. His leave will have been a few days short of 6 weeks.

STREISAND PERFORMING

September 15, New York, NY: The live performance of Barbra Streisand: A Happening in Central Park show aired on CBS. The open-air performance was the first live recording, in front of 135,000 spectators, for the singer.

HUMPHREY URGES MASSIVE U.S. AID TO COMBAT CRIME

September 16, Washington, DC: Vice President Humphrey published what he called a "serious, practical, detailed blueprint" for dealing with crime, largely through "massive" federal financial aid to the state and local police, courts, and correctional institutions.

LETTERS HOME FROM VIETNAM	CURRENT EVENTS

SEPTEMBER 18, VIETNAM

Dear Carol,

Fortunately, today was another light day. I only had 2 cases today and I really needed the break. I was so tired I just felt bad all over. I came back to my room and slept for a few hours and now I feel a lot better.

SEPTEMBER 20, VIETNAM

Dear Carol,

Today was still another one of those tough days, as I spent all day in the operating room. Today I got in a case of tetanus, which is the first I ever treated. I have seen this before, but I have never tried to treat this before. Unfortunately, I don't have everything I need to treat it.

GEORGE WALLACE NOMINATED

September 18, Texas: George C. Wallace accepted the presidential nomination of the American Party of Texas.

ABE FORTAS APPROVED BY SENATE PANEL FOR CHIEF JUSTICE

September 18, Washington, DC: By a vote of 11 to 6, the Senate Judiciary Committee approved President Johnson's nomination of Justice Abe Fortas to be chief justice of the United States.

HAWAII FIVE-O DEBUTS

September 20, Hollywood, CA: Hawaii Five-0 debuted on CBS, and eventually became the longest-running crime show in television history, until Law & Order overtook it in 2003.

NIXON VISITS SLUM AND MAKES WARNING TO WHITE COMMUNITY

September 21, Philadelphia, PA: Richard M. Nixon paid his first campaign visit to a Negro slum area and then toured the city, telling white suburbanites that they could not remain "an island in the world," indifferent to the plight of the urban and rural poor.

LETTERS HOME FROM VIETNAM

CURRENT EVENTS

SEPTEMBER 22, VIETNAM

Dear Carol,

Everyone is nervously awaiting the next big V.C. push, which according to our intelligence sources is supposed to be coming tonight. I hope nothing happens until Mac gets back. I have my hands full as it is, and the last thing I need is a big V.C. push right now. I still have not caught up from their push last week.

SEPTEMBER 24, VIETNAM

Dear Carol,

Well, Mac came back yesterday afternoon and this has already been a great help to me. I still had to do 3 procedures today, but he also had 3. So you see 3 are better than 6

SEPTEMBER 27, VIETNAM

Dear Carol,

I received a very sweet letter from you today. I'm glad that you enjoyed my little recording with Loc. That tape is certainly a treasure. Yes, I have worked out a system by which I can keep up with him. Before he left to go home with his mother, I gave him some books to read. These were Vietnamese story books and books to study. I promised him that if he read these I would give him more to read. I even promised him that I would send him books and clothes from time to time. This I intend to do even when I get back home.

200 WALK OUT AS CARDINAL UPHOLDS PAPAL EDICT ON BIRTH CURBS

September 22, Washington, DC: Two hundred Roman Catholics walked out of St. Matthew's Cathedral as their archbishop, Patrick Cardinal O'Boyle, began delivering a sermon urging obedience to Pope Paul VI's restrictions on birth control.

60 MINUTES DEBUTS

September 24, New York, NY: 60 Minutes debuted on CBS TV.

ABE FORTES NOMINATION SETBACK AS DIRKSEN HOLDS BACK SUPPORT

September 27, Washington, DC: The prospects for Justice Abe Fortas's confirmation as chief justice of the United States suffered a critical setback today when the Senate minority leader, Republican Everett Dirksen, dropped his strong advocacy of the nomination. Many see it as necessary for the nomination to succeed.

October 1968

LETTERS HOME FROM VIETNAM | **CURRENT EVENTS**

OCTOBER 10, VIETNAM

Dear Carol,

Today my old roommate, John Bohannon, came up from the subsector and we played a few sets of tennis. John beat me 6-4, 6-2, but I feel that this was pretty good considering the fact that John used to play on the West Point tennis team.

TIGERS WIN AND TAKE WORLD SERIES

October 10, Detroit, MI: The Detroit Tigers won the World Series by taking their third straight game from the St. Louis Cardinals, 4–1. Not even the great Bob Gibson could prevent it.

APOLLO LAUNCH

October 11, Cape Canaveral, FL: Apollo 7 launched from Florida for an 11-day journey that involved orbiting the Earth 163 times. The program was in preparation for a trip to the moon by NASA astronauts.

OCTOBER 14, VIETNAM

Dear Carol,

Things were a little more active for me today, as I did 4 cases, none of which were too bad. I guess we can strike off one more day now. Actually by the time you get this letter we will be into our 8th month. It feels like the 8th year.

OCTOBER 15, VIETNAM

Dear Carol,

Things here at the hospital are still quiet for me and I hope they stay that way for a while. Mac and I are still living together, working together, and playing tennis together.

APOLLO 7 TELECAST

October 14, Cape Canaveral, FL: Today marked the first live telecast from a manned U.S. spacecraft—Apollo 7.

HUMPHREY CONVINCED HE CAN WIN

October 14, Washington, DC: With a new and probably final burst of political energy, Humphrey set out to prove that his campaign was "coming alive" at last and that Richard M. Nixon could still be overtaken in a tight race over the next three weeks.

POLICE REJECT CONTRACT; P.B.A. VOTE TOO CLOSE

October 14, New York, NY: Delegates of the 22,000-member New York Patrolmen's Benevolent Association rejected a tentative two-year contract agreement reached with the city yesterday. Members resented the plan to put other forces, such as firemen and sanitation, on the same pay level and they rejected the contract terms.

HUMPHREY TAUNTS NIXON AS CHICKEN

October 15, St. Louis, MO: Mixing jest with political invective, Vice President Humphrey stumped through Missouri today, taunting "Richard the Chicken Hearted" to speak out on the issues and christening the Wallace-LeMay ticket "the Bombsy Twins."

LETTERS HOME FROM VIETNAM	CURRENT EVENTS

OCTOBER 21, VIETNAM

Dear Carol,

Would you believe that it is still raining like hell here? It has hardly let up for 48 hours. Everything is flooded like crazy and I am just thankful that I live on the third floor. Last night I had to go to the hospital (with MP protection) to do a C-section on a 20-year-old girl 8 months pregnant who had been shot in the abdomen. The bullet went right through the neck and head of the fetus. So after a quiet day I had an exciting night. When I finished that case last night I had to do a laparotomy on a teenage boy.

Well Darling, I received my absentee ballot today and I am definitely voting a straight Republican ticket. I hope you will join me in this, as I personally feel that under the circumstances, this is the wisest ticket to go with.

OCTOBER 22, VIETNAM

Dear Carol,

Activity here has picked up a little but not really too much. I hope it just stays quiet. I am afraid the V.C. are going to try something before the elections in the U.S.

NEW YORK CITY POLICE SICK CALLS REACH 2,000

October 21, New York, NY: Between 2,000 and 3,000 city policemen scheduled for duty reported sick as the Patrolmen's Benevolent Association pressed its drive for higher wages.

HUMPHREY URGES NEW YORKERS TO FIGHT HARDER

October 21, New York, NY: Vice President Humphrey campaigned in New York City for the fourth time in two weeks, lavishing special attention on the Jewish community and trying to bolster the party faithful with what he called a new sense of momentum. He said he was upset by anti-semitic comments being made during the city's school dispute with the union.

NIXON INTERFERES IN LBJ EFFORTS TO BEGIN PEACE TALKS

October 22, Washington, DC: During a phone call, Richard M. Nixon told his closest aide (and future chief of staff) H. R. Haldeman to "monkey wrench" President Lyndon B. Johnson's efforts to begin peace negotiations over the Vietnam War.

OCTOBER 27, VIETNAM

Dear Carol,

Today being Sunday I just went down to the hospital for a few hours, made rounds, did an amputation and then played tennis for 2 hours. I then went back to my room for a few hours of rest. This afternoon I returned to the tennis court and played for another 2 hours. So I had a big day on the tennis court. Mac is still sick and I am becoming a bit concerned. He really looks like hell and I just hope that he doesn't have something more than the flu.

OCTOBER 28, VIETNAM

Dear Carol,

Would you believe that another blue Monday is gone. Things are still a little on the quiet side. I will repeat, however, I like it that way. Every day that goes by is one more day that I do not have to go back to the hospital. Honey, by the time you get this letter, we will have about 24 more days until we will be together. We are still having counterpart trouble. That man has just been one frustration after another.

NEGROES READY TO JOIN DETROIT'S ECONOMY

October 27, Detroit, MI: Negroes in Detroit's slum area, the scene last year of the nation's worst racial riot, showed a new readiness to join the city's economic and social mainstream. Slum dwellers have become more aware of their progress.

FIREMEN CALL OFF WORK SLOWDOWN

October 28, New York, NY: The New York City Uniformed Firefighters Association followed the example set by the city's policemen and ordered its 10,500 members to end their five-day work slowdown. Michael J. Maye, the U.F.A.'s president, said the decision had been made because the union's delegates in the field had reported sentiment to reconsider a proposed labor contract with the city that was rejected by the rank and file last Monday.

LETTERS HOME FROM VIETNAM   **CURRENT EVENTS**

OCTOBER 30, VIETNAM

Dear Carol,

Things have picked up a little at the hospital but there still isn't too much activity in the province as far as the war is concerned. There is a lot of speculation as to why the V.C. are so quiet. Some feel that they are saving up for something really big. Others feel that they are honestly trying to establish some sort of peace. Still others feel that the V.C. are really hurting and are pulling back now for a long time. We will see.

THE QUEEN ELIZABETH RETIRED AS THOUSANDS LINED THE SHORE

October 30, New York Harbor, NY: Thousands of sentimental New Yorkers paid a noisy and colorful farewell to the largest passenger liner ever built, the Royal Mail Ship Queen Elizabeth, as she passed down river and headed out of the port for the last time.

MRS. ONASSIS PLANS TO FLY INTO NY IN TIME FOR VOTE ON TUESDAY

October 30, Athens, Greece: Aristotle S. Onassis, the Greek shipping millionaire, and his bride, the former Mrs. John F. Kennedy, have tentative plans to fly to New York in time for Mrs. Onassis to vote in the United States elections Tuesday.

November 1968

NOVEMBER 1, VIETNAM

Dear Carol,
I just received the news about the bombing halt. I certainly
hope that this means that a real peace is not far away. I pray
to God every night that this senseless war can come to an
end some way.

NOVEMBER 3, VIETNAM

Dear Carol,
Sunday night—We have gotten fairly busy at the hospital
again. Yesterday I did 2 laparotomies and 2 major
debridements. Today, Mac was on call and he did 4 majors.
The V.C. responded to our bombing halt by mortaring
the hell out of Vinh Long City last night. I hope that this
bombing halt doesn't backfire on us. It is now about 1:15
a.m. Monday morning and I can't sleep. Believe it or not I
have been sick again since Saturday night. This time I have
the intestinal flu.

NOVEMBER 5, VIETNAM

Dear Carol,
I am feeling better now. Today we were busy as hell as Mac
and I did 5 cases each. I still don't know what to make of the
bombing halt. I pray that it isn't disastrous.

NIXON LINKS RIVAL TO "SECURITY GAP"

November 1, San Antonio, TX: Richard M. Nixon chose the home state of Lyndon B. Johnson to say Humphrey is a "fuzzy thinker" and to restate in harsher language his charge of a week ago that the president had permitted "a security gap" to develop in the nation's military strength relative to that of the Soviet Union.

NY EMPLOYEES LEAVE COLUMBIA

November 3, Morningside Heights, NY: The 75 Columbia University employees who had staged a sit-in at the university president's office left during the night.

ELECTION DAY NEWS

November 5, Washington, DC: The results of the presidential election's showed the popular vote split as 31,770,000 for Nixon, 43.4 percent of the total; 31,270,000 or 42.7 percent for Humphrey; 9,906,000 or 13.5 percent for Wallace; and 0.4 percent for other candidates.

| LETTERS HOME FROM VIETNAM | CURRENT EVENTS |

NOVEMBER 6, VIETNAM

Dear Carol,

We have been following the election coverage. Boy is that close, far closer than I ever expected. The Vietnamese are really pulling for Nixon. They are scared that Humphrey will pull the U.S. out of Vietnam. They are very displeased with the bombing halt. There is, however, mixed feelings amongst the American GIs. I too have mixed emotions about the bombing halt. Things are really back in full swing. In the last 2 days Mac and I have done a total of 23 major cases in 2 days. There has definitely been an increase in activity since the bombing halt.

NOVEMBER 8, VIETNAM

Dear Carol,

Things are still relatively busy at the hospital. I have had a run on laparotomies lately and fortunately they are all doing OK so far. Surgery is fun in moderate doses, but I must confess that this is getting a bit old.

THIN MARGIN MAKES NIXON WINNER

November 6, Washington, DC: Headlines reported that Richard M. Nixon won the presidential election by a thin margin. He pleaded for the nation to reunite.

HUMPHREY MET NIXON IN FLORIDA AND PLEDGED SUPPORT

November 8, Opa-locka, FL: In an amiable display of bipartisan unity, president-elect Richard M. Nixon and the man he defeated for the presidency three days earlier, Vice President Humphrey, met to exchange assurances of support.

CATHOLIC BISHOPS WILL ACT ON BIRTH CONTROL AND WAR

November 11, Benton Harbor, MI: The Roman Catholic bishops in America moved toward a possible effort to ease the consciences of Catholic couples who cannot accept the papal ban on artificial contraception. Their conference hinted at a softer stand on the papal encyclical.

NOVEMBER 12, VIETNAM

Dear Carol,

I am enclosing a note I received from one of the nurses at the hospital. Can you read it? This note is a classic and I want to save it. This depicts a problem that is quite unique to this part of the world. I certainly hate to take pleasure in another's misfortune, but I must confess that I got a few chuckles out of this (a water buffalo injuring a person in the rectum). It's a problem that you just don't see in the U.S. If you get a chance, show this to Bob Yoder. I am sure he would get a kick out of it. Well today was busy as hell. I had 2 laparotomies and 2 big debridements and I am tired. I just can't wait to get away from this place.

NOVEMBER 13, VIETNAM

Dear Carol,

I just can't believe we are so busy. The number of war casualties is just unbelievable. There are so many, I just can't operate on all of them. I am so damn tired I can't believe it. R&R just couldn't come at a better time. You will probably get this letter about 2 days before you leave.

SUPREME COURT ENDS ARKANSAS BAN ON DARWINISM

November 12, Washington, DC: The Supreme Court concluded the nation's second monkey trial today by declaring unconstitutional an Arkansas law that made it a crime to teach Charles Darwin's theory of evolution in the public schools.

WOMEN ADMITTED TO YALE

November 13, New Haven, CT: Yale University announced that it will admit women for the first time.

KU KLUX KLAN AND THREE MEN FINED $1 MILLION IN SLAYING OF NEGRO IN MISSISSIPPI

November 13, Vicksburg, MS: A federal district court judge returned a $1,021,500 judgment against the White Knights of the Ku Klux Klan and three Natchez white men for the slaying of an aged Negro, Ben Chester White, in 1966.

LETTERS HOME FROM VIETNAM   **CURRENT EVENTS**

NOVEMBER 15, VIETNAM

Dear Carol,
I wrote you a letter last night and walked out without mailing it. I will send you two letters tonight. I am very tired so I will be brief. The war casualties are coming in at a rate that is greater than at any time since I have been here. R&R is really coming at the right time, because I have gotten into another one of those states of pure exhaustion. I am really tired of this place and these people and the whole damn war.

NOVEMBER 16, VIETNAM

Dear Carol,
Things are still real busy over here. We have really had a run on laparotomies. I have never seen so many bad abdominal injures. The Vietnamese Regional Forces, similar to our National Guard, just received a big shipment of M-16 rifles and I believe they are just shooting up the countryside. As I said before, this R&R is really coming at a good time. I still don't know if I'll be in Honolulu on the 24th or the 25th.

PRESIDENT JOHNSON WILL NOT SHARE POLICY DECISIONS WITH NIXON BEFORE INAUGURATION

November 15, Washington, DC: President Johnson made clear that Richard M. Nixon would not have any decision-making role in foreign affairs before the January 20 inauguration, although he did welcome consultation. The role as foreign policy maker is still the president's.

"LOVE CHILD" HITS NO. 1

November 16, Detroit, MI: Diana Ross and the Supremes' "Love Child" hit number 1 on the best-selling charts.

December 1968

DECEMBER 11, VIETNAM

Dear Carol,

We are still busy and as usual, we are spending most of our day in surgery. The casualties continue to pour in and we continue to operate. I guess I can take it for 85 more days. I guess I can put up with anything for 85 more days. By the time you get this letter, I will have 90 more days in country and I will spend the last week in Saigon. I even love to talk about leaving this dreadful place.

DECEMBER 20, VIETNAM

Dear Carol,

I was certainly glad to hear that the Pueblo crew is going to be released. Now I just wish that we could bring an end to this awful war over here. Today I gave the camera to Bo Huong and Charlie, and boy were they ever happy. I just hope that they can afford to buy film and have it developed. We are having a MILPHAP Christmas Party tomorrow night, but I must say that it is quite difficult to get the real Christmas spirit over here. Vietnam just isn't very Christmassy.

UNEMPLOYMENT RISES

December 11, Washington, DC: The unemployment rate, at 3.3 percent, was reported as the lowest it has been in 15 years.

JOHNSON PREDICTS A BUDGET SURPLUS AS TAX FUNDS RISE

December 20, Washington, DC: President Johnson reported that the federal budget for the present fiscal year is expected to show a small surplus.

PUEBLO CREW RELEASED

December 23, Washington, DC: The White House reported that the crew of the USS Pueblo had been released, after spending 11 months in captivity by the North Koreans.

LETTERS HOME FROM VIETNAM

CURRENT EVENTS

DECEMBER 23, VIETNAM

Dear Carol,

I sure am happy for the crew of the Pueblo. That was some Christmas present they received. As a matter of fact, today was a real good day for the U.S. as our moon shot seems to be going well. I just hope that these guys are back OK that whole flight is absolutely amazing. Not too much news here . . . everything is about the same. Everyone is looking toward next month, with caution, as the Tet Lunar New Year will be coming soon. When that is over, I know that everyone will be quite relieved.

DECEMBER 24, VIETNAM

Dear Carol,

I'm getting ready to go to bed and I just wanted to drop you a note to tell you that I love you. I am going down to Vinh Long in the morning. There are a lot of brave men over here and my assignment compared to theirs is peaches and cream. Saigon is noisy tonight, as I can hear mortar fire all over the place. This happens every night and I am just about to get to the point where it doesn't bother me too much.

JERSEY MAFIA SCANDAL TRACED TO NEW YORK PROHIBITION GANGS

December 23, Trenton, NJ: The Mafia activity reported recently in New Jersey has its roots in the bathtub gin days of the bootlegging nineteen-twenties and the labor racketeering of the thirties, according to law-enforcement agents. Present day Mafia leaders can trace their background to the 1920s gangs that brought into the state bootleg booze.

APOLLO 8 ORBITS MOON

December 24, Houston, TX: Apollo 8 entered an orbit around the moon. Astronauts Frank Borman, Jim Lovell, and William Anders become the first humans to see the far side of the moon and the planet Earth as a whole. The crew read from Genesis.

THE CREW OF THE PUEBLO GREETED

December 24, San Diego, CA: The crew of the intelligence ship Pueblo returned to the United States in time for Christmas with many of their families.

DECEMBER 25, VIETNAM

Dear Carol,

Merry Christmas! I spent my Christmas making rounds at the hospital this morning and then playing tennis for about 3 hours this morning. Then we had a Christmas dinner this afternoon followed by a few drinks. Presently there is a band upstairs supplying music for the party tonight. Everyone has spent the entire day daydreaming about home. Maybe next year let's hope. How did you spend your Christmas?

DECEMBER 27, VIETNAM

Dear Carol,

By the time you get this letter it should be January. Do you remember last January? We were just starting to get nervous as hell about Vietnam. We were also making plans to move. Exactly one year ago today we were in San Francisco. As a matter of fact, it was one year ago today that I stopped smoking. How about that! I am very proud of that.

APOLLO 8 COMPLETES 10 REVOLUTIONS AROUND MOON

December 25, Houston, TX: The Apollo 8 astronauts flew around the moon 10 times and photographed the desolate area of the surface before starting their return to Earth.

200,000 WITHOUT HEAT AT CHRISTMAS IN NEW YORK CITY

December 25, New York, NY: With temperatures dropping to 12 degrees during the early hours of Christmas day, it was reported that many homes had not received heating oil due to a deliverers' strike when drivers refused to deliver during holiday period. Some did receive oil, but only when drivers were paid two and a half times their usual hourly rate.

APOLLO 8 LANDING

December 27, Houston, TX: Apollo 8, the first manned mission to the moon, made a safe nighttime splashdown in the Pacific Ocean.

| LETTERS HOME FROM VIETNAM | CURRENT EVENTS |

DECEMBER 28, VIETNAM

Dear Carol,
It is Saturday night, very late and I am getting ready to
go to bed. Although the mail doesn't go out until Monday
morning, I just wanted to drop you a note anyway. Today I
was busy at the hospital. A V.C. terror squad placed a bomb
in a school classroom and it really messed a few people up
pretty badly. However, I think I have learned to relax a little
more now. I just do the most I can, the best I can, and I
don't seem to worry about all this quite as much. It is still so
depressing and so far removed from reality as we know it.

MIAMI POP FESTIVAL

December 28, Miami FL:
One hundred thousand people
attended Miami Pop Festival.
The same day, the Beatles' White
Album went to number 1 on the
record charts and remained there
for nine weeks.

DECEMBER 31, VIETNAM

Dear Carol,
Today I got my first set of slides back and with the exception
of 3, they were not too bad. As a matter of fact, most of them
were pretty good. I think that before I leave I should be able
to accumulate quite a collection of interesting slides.

Would you believe that here we are in the dry season and
it is raining like hell outside. Everything in Vietnam is
unpredictable. Well, Baby, I am going to say Happy New
Year. Remember that I love you very much and that I will be
home very soon.

NEW HAVEN RR SOLD TO PENN CENTRAL RAIL FOR $146 MILLION

**December 31, New Haven,
CT:** The New Haven Railroad, a
threadbare bankrupt railroad
with erratic schedules, shrinking
rolling stock, and dirty stations,
was absorbed into the prosperous
Penn Central system.

January 1969

JANUARY 2, VIETNAM

Dear Carol,

Today was really a big one for us here in Vinh Long. One of the helicopter pilots accidently fired a bunch of rockets right into the middle of town. People were killed immediately. 2 more died at the hospital and 2 more probably will die. I took 2 of them to surgery and Mac took 2. We ended up the day today doing 6 major cases each. I certainly hope that this is no indication as to what the coming year will be like.

JANUARY 3, VIETNAM

Dear Carol,

I am afraid that today was another one of those depressing days, as I didn't get any mail from you. Mac will be leaving for his R&R to Formosa on January 16 and should be back around January 26. So that will be a bad 10 days there.

HENRY CABOT LODGE NOMINATED BY NIXON

January 2, Washington, DC: Henry Cabot Lodge, former American ambassador to South Vietnam, was nominated by president-elect Nixon to be the senior U.S negotiator at the Paris Peace Talks.

JOHN LENNON AND YOKO ONO ARRESTED IN NEWARK

January 3, Newark, NJ: A new album by John Lennon called Two Virgins and featuring John Lennon and Yoko Ono in the nude was confiscated at Newark Airport. The album was not allowed to be sold in the United States.

LETTERS HOME FROM VIETNAM　　　　　　**CURRENT EVENTS**

JANUARY 11, VIETNAM

Dear Carol,

Well here it is Saturday night and this of course means that another dreadful week has come to an end. Honey, the time is really getting short and so is my attitude. I feel that I have given enough and I am tired. I am trying to cut back on the amount of surgery that I will be doing and am trying to increase the load of my counterpart even more. I absolutely refuse to begin a case that might keep me at the hospital after dark. So you see I really am getting the short term syndrome.

We have not been playing tennis lately with both Mac and I being sick. Not only that we have been spending some of our free time taking pictures. As I am sure you have gathered, I am really having a ball with the camera. I am accumulating a rather nice collection of slides.

MILLIONS IN CITY POVERTY FUNDS LOST

January 11, New York, NY: As a result of multiple investigations, it has been reported that evidence points to New York City's $122 million-a-year antipoverty program has been plagued by chronic corruption and administrative chaos that have already cheated New York's poor of uncounted millions of dollars.

NY JETS GET UPSET VICTORY OVER BALTIMORE IN SUPER BOWL

January 12, Miami, FL: In a memorable upset that astonished virtually everyone in the football realm, the New York Jets of the American League beat the Baltimore Colts, the supposedly indomitable National League champions, 16–7, in Super Bowl III.

JANUARY 13, VIETNAM

Dear Carol,

I have been quite busy lately, as I have had a run on belly injuries. They are a lot of hard work but they keep the time going by. I work now pretty much out of habit, my mind is with you. Well that's about it for now. I will say goodnight here. When you get this letter, we will be entering our 11th month. It isn't long now.

JANUARY 17, VIETNAM

Dear Carol,

So things have been quiet since Mac has been gone, although he has only been gone 2 days. I know better than to expect things to stay quiet until he gets back. Today I only had 3 cases, although one of these was a tough femoral artery repair. However, if I don't have to do more than 3 cases each day, I really can't complain.

PRESIDENT JOHNSON SAYS THE PEOPLE GAINED IN HIS PRESIDENCY

January 13, New York, NY: At a reception hosted by Governor Rockefeller at the Plaza Hotel, President Johnson said that "what really matters is not the ultimate judgment that historians will pass" on his administration "but whether there was a change for the better in the way our people live." He believed that he had made great inroads into helping the poor and American students, and in ensuring the civil rights of all citizens.

U.S. ACCUSES IBM OF MONOPOLIZING COMPUTER MARKET

January 17, Washington, DC: The Justice Department announced that it had filed suit against the giant International Business Machines Corporation, alleging it monopolized the $3 billion general purpose digital computer market. The suit charged the company with preventing competition in the digital equipment field. The Justice Department indicated that it would seek at least a partial breakup of the company.

LETTERS HOME FROM VIETNAM

CURRENT EVENTS

JANUARY 18, VIETNAM

Dear Carol,

You don't have to apologize for being scared. Honey I am scared too and I have been since I have been over here. Things are relatively quiet in Vinh Long Province as compared with the other provinces in the delta, which are hot as hell right now. Yes, everyone is quite tense in anticipation of a Tet Offensive. Yes, Darling, I will be very careful. I just have faith that the God who has looked over us for 10 months will continue to do so and bring me back home safely to you. Honey, just try not to worry too much. Just remember that soon this will all be over with. I assure you that I am OK and that I will be very careful.

WINSLOW HOMER DISPLAY

January 18, Washington, DC:
The Smithsonian, in Washington, DC, opened a display of American artist Winslow Homer for a six-week engagement.

JANUARY 25, VIETNAM

Dear Carol,

Not really too much news here. Everyone is still quite tense in anticipation of the up coming Tet Lunar New Year. Most people seem to feel that the V.C. do not have the strength now to pull off an offensive of the magnitude that characterized the last Tet Offensive. Well we will soon find out. At any rate, I think that our people are more prepared for such an offensive this year.

GEORGE ROMNEY APPOINTS TWO NEGROES TO POSITIONS

January 25, Washington, DC:
George Romney, secretary of Housing and Urban Development, announced he had made five key appointments in his department, including two prominent Negroes, Samuel C. Jackson and Samuel J. Simmons. Both men were prominent members of the NAACP.

JANUARY 29, VIETNAM

Dear Carol,

Mac is still gone and I am still carrying the load by myself. Things are not quite as busy as they were last time he went off, but they seem to be picking up this week. I am back up to doing 5 and 6 major cases each day. It tires hell out of me, but it makes the time go by.

JANUARY 30, VIETNAM

Dear Carol,

Everyone is really tense around here with Tet coming up. Believe me I would rather it be like this. I am sure that if something happens this year, no one will be taken by surprise. As I have said before, I will be OK, there is someone watching over us.

JANUARY 31, VIETNAM

Dear Carol,

Well . . . today I celebrated my birthday by having a real knock down drag out argument with my counterpart. Honey, I am a real "hot head" and I know it and I am not proud of it, but sometimes I just can't help it. However, I do have one attribute that I am proud of and that being that I am not afraid to stand up for what I think is right. I have always been a man of high principle, at least I have tried to be, and when the day comes that I start compromising my principles, I will essentially be nothing.

PRESIDENT NIXON PLANS TOUR OF WESTERN EUROPE

January 29, Washington, DC: **Preside**nt Nixon announced plans to tour Western European capitals during his first months in office. The goal was to assure members of the western alliance that the United States has their support.

CREDIT FOR ROTC TO END AT YALE

January 30, New Haven, CT: The Yale College faculty voted to strip the Reserve Officers Training Corps of its academic standing at the college and relegate it to the status of an extracurricular activity.

NIXON BACKS A PLAN TO JAIL SUSPECTS HELD IN CRIME-PRONE AREAS

January 31, Washington, DC: President Nixon endorsed the controversial concept of preventive detention for "hard-core" criminal suspects as part of a broad program to reduce crime and alleviate poverty in the nation's capital.

February 1969

FEBRUARY 12, VIETNAM

Dear Carol,

Well I guess that's enough chatter for now. I am going to say goodnight for now. By the way, I want you to know that I am being ultra careful. Tonight my counterpart had a big Tet Party at the hospital. We are on 24 hours alert and no one is supposed to be out of the compound after 6:00 p.m. The team got permission to go anyway, but I declined. They can have all the parties they want. I just want to come home. You and I can have our own little party then . . . OK?

TROOPS SENT TO UNIVERSITY OF WISCONSIN

February 12, Madison, WI: Governor Warren P. Knowles ordered 900 Wisconsin National Guard troops to the University of Wisconsin campus in Madison after 3,000 students disrupted classes for the fourth day. The governor's action came in the wake of arrests and violence on the fifth day of a student strike in support of 13 nonnegotiable black demands, including the establishment of an autonomous black studies department.

SIRHAN BARS PLEA, PREFERS FULL TRIAL

February 12, Los Angeles: Sirhan Bishara Sirhan met with his lawyers in the jail at the Hall of Justice and decided to retain his plea of not guilty to first-degree murder in the slaying of Senator Robert F. Kennedy.

LETTERS HOME FROM VIETNAM   **CURRENT EVENTS**

FEBRUARY 14, VIETNAM

Dear Carol,

Not much new here, except for the fact that we are 1 day closer to being together. I figure that I have about 22 days left in Vinh Long City. I will feel half way home when I get out of here and get to Tan Son Nhut. There are all kinds of parties going on around here in celebration of the Tet New Year. I have not attended any of them and I don't intend to. I have the rest of my life to party. I will wait until I get out of here before I go off partying. You and I can have a big party when I get back.

I received a letter today from the Ohio Medical license board with instructions concerning what I have to do to get my Ohio license. The main thing I have to do is to pay them $100 and get a bunch of reference letters. I can take care of all this when I return to B'ham.

FEBRUARY 17, VIETNAM

Dear Carol,

By my calculations, I have 19 days remaining here in Vinh Long. So now that coming home day is really getting close. I have been telling everyone that I am too short to get into a long conversation. Being short is fun, but it's also scary. Today is the first day of Tet and of course no one is working today. One of the army officers, stationed in a small outpost just outside of town about 15 miles, asked Mac and I to ride out with him to see his outpost. Mac went but my better judgment told me to stay right here in the compound and right here I am. With 19 days left, I just can't see taking an unnecessary chance like that. Actually it really doesn't make good sense regardless of how many days are left. If there were a good valid medical reason to go out there, I would not hesitate. However, this isn't a very healthy country to go

SIRHAN DEFENSE CONTENDS HE KILLED WHILE IN TRANCE

February 14, Los Angeles, CA: An attorney for Sirhan Bishara Sirhan said that when Sirhan killed Senator Robert F. Kennedy, a man he "admired and loved," he was "out of contact with reality, in a trance."

INDUSTRY OUTPUT AND G.N.P. UP, BUT AMOUNT OF INCREASE NARROWS

February 14, Washington, DC: Industrial production continued to rise in January, but less strongly than in most other recent months, the Federal Reserve Board reported today.

NATIONAL GUARD REDUCED AT UNIVERSITY OF WISCONSIN

February 17, Madison, WI: Some of the 1,900 National Guardsmen called up to quell disturbances at the University of Wisconsin were sent home despite a resumption of disruptive tactics by hundreds of student strikers demanding a black studies department. Students were accused of demonstrating in classrooms and pulling fire alarms. The situation calmed enough for a substantial number of guardsmen to be allowed to leave for home.

sightseeing. Most of this week will be holidays, which means very little work. However, the days will certainly drag like never before. By the time you get this letter I will be down to 2 weeks so I guess the time is going by. Well baby, I'm going to say goodbye for now.

OIL DRILLERS HELD LIABLE FOR SLICKS

February 17, Washington, DC: Secretary of the Interior Walter J. Hickel today made oil companies responsible for cleaning up any pollution resulting from offshore oil drilling operations. Hickel wants oil companies to clean up spills even if it cannot be proven they were the cause. This was the first Federal action taken to deal with the issue since an oil slick from a Union Oil Company spill along the Santa Barbara Channel off the California coastline, which covered beaches and killed wildlife.

FEBRUARY 20, VIETNAM

Dear Carol,
Today was quite full of aggravation (more than usual) and quite a bit of work. So I am really all worn out.

POLICEMAN TESTIFIES SIRHAN WAS NOT INTOXICATED WHEN HE SHOT KENNEDY

February 20, Los Angeles, CA: A policeman declared today that in his opinion Sirhan Bishara Sirhan was not intoxicated, as the defense has said it will prove, when he shot Senator Robert F. Kennedy.

LETTERS HOME FROM VIETNAM   **CURRENT EVENTS**

FEBRUARY 23, VIETNAM

Dear Carol,

I will leave Vinh Long two weeks from today. The very thought of leaving Vinh Long just makes me feel good all over. I just hope that things are quiet in the Saigon area, so I don't have any difficulty getting out of there. I still can't believe that this is for real, that this nightmare is really almost over with. I am sure that by now you have heard about the new nationwide offensive. Well, let me assure you that I am OK. So far all the fighting is out in the rural areas. It is still not known how big of an offensive this will turn out to be. I promise I am being ultra-careful.

FEBRUARY 24, VIETNAM

Dear Carol,

Not really too much more to say for now. We are still waiting to see what magnitude this offensive will reach. So far the Americans all over the country are coming out quite well. Let's just keep our prayers coming and our fingers crossed.

FEBRUARY 25, VIETNAM

Dear Carol,

One more day down and now only 11 days left in Vinh Long. With this new offensive it looks like there are going to be some busy days, at least the last 2 days have been quite busy. However, all the activity is out in the rural areas and let's just hope that it stays there.

12,000 COAL MINERS JOIN WILDCAT STRIKE

February 23, W. Virginia: Between 12,000 and 15,000 coal miners in southern West Virginia joined a wildcat strike to press for compensation for men who contract the miners disease known as black lung.

NEW YORK CITY PLANS TO HIRE YOUNG PEOPLE IN SLUMS AS POLICE CADETS

February 24, New York, NY: New York City announced plans to use federal, state, and city funds to train Brooklyn slum youths as police cadets and private guards for residents and merchants in their communities.

NEGRO TELLS STATE HEARING NYACK, NEW YORK FIRE UNIT BARS HIM

February 25, Nyack, NY: A 22-year-old machinist started state proceedings against a volunteer fire company and several of its officials, charging he had been denied membership because he is a Negro.

March 1969

MARCH 2, VIETNAM

Dear Carol,

Today I am beginning my last week here in Vinh Long. In exactly one week I will be leaving here and in exactly two weeks I will be home with you. No Honey, no one will forward my mail to Saigon. It will only be forwarded home. So stop writing, OK. You have done an excellent job, but it is now time to stop.

MARCH 6, VIETNAM

Dear Carol,

I am in the process of finishing up some last minute details before I leave. Coming home involves a lot of red tape, but this is one time that I don't mind going through red tape. I guess I could put up with most anything.

MANTLE ENDS 18-YEAR INJURY-RIDDEN BASEBALL CAREER

March 2, Ft. Lauderdale, FL: Mickey Mantle, the 37-year-old New York Yankee slugger, announced his retirement after 18 injury-ridden seasons in big league baseball. "I can't hit when I need to," he said at the Yanks' spring training base in Fort Lauderdale.

PAINE NAMED BY NIXON AS ADMINISTRATOR OF NASA

March 6, Washington, DC: President Nixon today named Dr. Thomas O. Paine, a scientist, administrator, and World War II submarine officer, to head the nation's civilian space program.

Acknowledgments

Headlines and stories for "Events in the United States:"
https://timesmachine.nytimes.com

Photographs:
A mixture of photographs from Dr. Sheldon Kushner
and Dr. James (Mac) McComb

DuSable Museum used with permission
by Antonio Vernon, Director, Chicago WikiProject

Bart Starr photos courtesy of Getty Images.

Endnotes

[1] The term *war baby* refers to a child born in wartime, especially during World War I or World War II. This is not to be confused with *baby boomers*, a term referring to those who are part of the phenomenon of increased births in post–World War II America (see "War Baby," Dictionary.com, www.dictionary.com/browse/war-baby). The expression "boom" was first used in May 1951, by Sylvia Porter, a columnist for the *New York Post*.

[2] Dr. Sheldon Kushner, interview with the author, January 2017. All subsequently cited interviews with Sheldon were conducted by the author.

[3] Dr. Sheldon Kushner, interview, July 2013.

[4] Dr. Sheldon Kushner, interview, October 2012.

[5] Dr. Sheldon Kushner, interview, November 2016.

[6] Dr. Sheldon Kushner, interview, October 2016.

[7] Jennifer Rosenbert, "Rosa Parks Refuses to Give Up Her Bus Seat," About.com. Clifford and Virginia Durr were white supporters of the civil rights movement in Montgomery, Alabama, and helped to provide bail money to get Rosa Parks out of jail after a family friend called to tell him she had been arrested.

[8] Ibid.

[9] Dr. Sheldon Kushner, quoting his brother Dr. Jack Kushner in an interview, November 2014.

[10] Dr. Sheldon Kushner, quoting his brother Harold Kushner in an interview, November 2014.

[11] Dr. Sheldon Kushner, interview, November 2014.

[12] Ibid.

[13] *Chicago Tribune*, obituary posted December 11, 1987: "Eugene Pieter Romayn Feldman, 65, one of the founders in the early 1960s of the Du Sable Museum of African American History, served as its director of development and planning for many years. He also wrote many pamphlets on black history. In more recent years, he has served the museum as a researcher and archivist. A memorial ceremony for Mr. Feldman, who had moved back to Montgomery, Ala., after 26 years here, will be held at a later date at the DuSable Museum, 740 E. 56th Pl. He died Nov. 29 at home in Montgomery."

[14] Dr. Sheldon Kushner, interview, November 2014.

[15] Dr. Sheldon Kushner, interview, November 2014.

[16] Houston Methodist, www.houstonmethodist.org/heart-vascular.

[17] Dr. Sheldon Kushner, interview, August 2015.

[18] Ibid.

[19] Dr. Sheldon Kushner, interview, July 2013.

[20] Ibid.

[21] Ibid.

[22] Sheldon Kushner, interview, October 2016.

[23] Ibid.

[24] The Berry Plan is named after Frank Berry a prominent thoracic surgeon and Harvard graduate who was appointed as the second assistant secretary of defense (health affairs) in 1954. Upon assuming office, Berry proposed a plan for young military physicians to follow one of three pathways after completing their internship:

1. Enter the armed services immediately and return to their residencies after fulfilling their obligated service

2. Enter the armed services two years after medical school and complete their residencies after service

3. Enter the service after the completion of residency training

The Berry Plan deferred doctors who were taking their residency, so that the Army would get the benefit of their advanced education (see F. B. Berry, "The Story of the Berry Plan, *Bulletin of the New York Academy of Medicine* 52, no. 3 (March–April 1976): 278–282, www.ncbi.nlm.nih.gov/pmc/articles/PMC1808239/).

[25] Dr. Sheldon Kushner, interview, October 2016.

[26] Ibid.

[27] The Tet Offensive was launched in January–February 1968 by the Viet Cong and the North Vietnamese army. Timed to coincide with the first day of the Tet (Vietnamese New Year), it was a surprise attack on South Vietnamese cities, notably Saigon. Although repulsed after initial successes, the attack shook U.S. confidence and hastened the withdrawal of its forces (see "Tet Offensive," History.com, www.history.com/topics/vietnam-war/tet-offensive).

[28] "Tan Son Nhut Air Base (Vietnamese: C n c không quân Tân S n Nh t) (1955–1975) was a Republic of Vietnam Air Force (VNAF) facility. It is located near the city of Saigon in southern Vietnam. The United States used it as a major base during the Vietnam War (1959–1975), stationing Army, Air Force, Navy, and Marine units there. Following the Fall of Saigon, it was taken over as a Vietnam People's Air Force (VPAF) facility and remains in use today" ("Tan Son Nhut Air Base," Wikipedia, en.wikipedia.org/wiki/Tan_Son_Nhut_Air_Base).

[29] Dr. Sheldon Kushner, interview, August 2015.

[30] Ibid.

[31] Philip F. Napoli, *Bringing It All Back Home: An Oral History of New York City's Vietnam Veterans* (New York: Hill & Wang, 2013), 25.

[32] Dr. Sheldon Kushner, letter, March 22, 1968.

[33] Dr. Sheldon Kushner, letter, March 23, 1968.

[34] Harvey Meyerson, *Vinh Long* (Boston: Houghton Mifflin Company, 1970), 93 and 207.

[35] Lam Quang Thi, *The Twenty-Five Year Century* (Denton: University of North Texas Press, 2002), 182.

[36] A rice bowl is an area that produces a large quantity of rice ("Rice Bowl," OxfordDictionaries.com, en.oxforddictionaries.com/definition/rice_bowl).

[37] Va-Tong Xuan, "Rice Cultivation in the Mekong Delta," *South East Asian Studies* 13, no. 1 (June 1975), kyoto-seas.org/pdf/13/1/130106.pdf.

[38] Robert J. Wilensky, *Military Medicine to Win Hearts and Minds: Aid to Civilians in the Vietnam War* (Lubbock: Texas Tech University Press, 2004), 86.

[39] Ibid, p. 76.

[40] Ibid, p. 66.

[41] Department of the Army, "Vietnam Studies: Medical Support 1965–1970," Chapter XIII, p. 163, found at www.history.army.mil/html/books/090/90-16/CMH_Pub_90-16.pdf

[42] Wilinsky, *Military Medicine*, p. 67.

[43] Major General Spurgeon Neel, *Medical Support of the U.S. Army in Vietnam 1965–1970* (Washington DC: U.S. Government Printing Office, 1973), www.history.army.mil/html/books/090/90-16/index.html.

[44] Ibid.

[45] The Volunteer Physicians for Vietnam program was administered by the American Medical Association and financed by the State Department's Agency for International Development (see the abstract of "Volunteer Physicians for Vietnam," *JAMA* 219, no. 4 (1972), jamanetwork.com/journals/jama/article-abstract/340641).

[46] Dr. Sheldon Kushner, interview, November 2014.

[47] Dr. Sheldon Kushner, interview, October 2016.

[48] Tom Graue, medic, interview with the author, June 2012. All interviews with Tom Graue were conducted by the author.

[49] Dr. Sheldon Kushner, interview, August 2015. Fred continued to practice pediatrics in Tennessee after returning from Vietnam (Dr. Sheldon Kushner, interview, October 2016).

[50] James Gordon McComb, MD, is based in Los Angeles, California, and his medical specialization is neurological surgery. He attended the University of Miami Medical School and interned in pediatrics at UCLA. When he returned to the States after serving in Vinh Long, he entered his residency in pediatric neurosurgery at Massachusetts General Hospital, which is affiliated with Harvard University. He subsequently became a pediatric neurosurgeon in Los Angeles. Today Dr. McComb continues to practice neurosurgery in Los Angeles, and he is affiliated with Children's Hospital Los Angeles, Keck Hospital of USC, and Huntington Memorial Hospital. He is one of two doctors at Children's Hospital Los Angeles and one of 13 at Huntington Memorial Hospital who specialize in neurological surgery. He also has published many important articles in his field (see www.chla.org/profile/j-gordon-mccomb-md).

[51] Dr. Sheldon Kushner, interview, August 2015.

[52] Tom Graue, interview, June 2012.

[53] Dr. Sheldon Kushner, interview, January 2017.

[54] Dr. Sheldon Kushner, letter, March 30, 1968. What Sheldon describes reflects the influence of the French way of structuring the work day, originating from the time they occupied Vietnam, until their defeat in 1954.

[55] Dr. Sheldon Kushner, interview, November 2014.

[56] *North Vietnamese regulars* refers to the army of uniformed soldiers fighting for North Vietnam. *Viet Cong* were part of the communist guerrilla movement in Vietnam that fought the South Vietnamese government forces from 1954 to 1975 with the support of the North Vietnamese army and opposed the South Vietnamese and U.S. forces in the Vietnam War. *Guerillas* refers to members of a small independent group taking part in irregular fighting, typically against larger regular forces (see "North Vietnamese Regulars Are Fighting in South Vietnam," History.com, www.history.com/this-day-in-history/north-vietnamese-regulars-are-fighting-in-south-vietnam, and "Vietnam War," HistoryNet, www.historynet.com/vietnam-war, among other places).

[57] Dr. Sheldon Kushner, letter, August 26, 1968.

[58] Dr. Sheldon Kushner, tape recording, September 1968.

[59] Ibid.

[60] Dr. Sheldon Kushner, letter, April 4, 1968.

[61] Dr. Sheldon Kushner, letter, April 19, 1968.

[62] Hepatitis is a swelling and inflammation of the liver. It is not a condition but often refers to a viral infection of the liver ("Hepatitis," Merriam-Webster, www.merriam-webster.com/dictionary/hepatitis).

[63] Gamma globulin is a type of protein found in the blood. When gamma globulins are extracted from the blood of many people and combined, they can be used to prevent or treat infections (see "Gammaglobulin," Encyclopedia.com, www.encyclopedia.com/medicine/anatomy-and-physiology/anatomy-and-physiology/gammaglobulin).

[64] Dr. Sheldon Kushner, letter, June 14, 1968.

[65] Dr. Sheldon Kushner, letter, November 12, 1968.

[66] Dr. Sheldon Kushner, interview, July 2013.

[67] Sheldon Kushner, letter, July 2, 1968.

[68] Sheldon Kushner, letter, July 3, 1968.

[69] Sheldon Kushner, letter, September 14, 1968.

[70] Ibid.

[71] Sheldon Kushner, letter, August 25, 1968.

[72] Sheldon Kushner, interview, August 2015.

[73] Dr. Sheldon Kushner, letter, May 15, 1968.

[74] Dr. Sheldon Kushner, letter, May 17, 1968.

[75] Dr. Sheldon Kushner, letter, August 25, 1968.

[76] Dr. Sheldon Kushner, letter, April 10, 1968.

[77] Dr. Sheldon Kushner, letter, May 6, 1968.

[78] Dr. Sheldon Kushner, letter, August 8, 1968.

[79] Dr. Sheldon Kushner, interview, July 2013.

[80] Dr. Sheldon Kushner, interview, July 2013.

[81] A laparotomy is a surgical incision into the abdominal cavity (see "Laparotomy," The Free Dictionary, medical-dictionary.thefreedictionary.com/laparotomy)

[82] Dr. Sheldon Kushner, letter, October 21, 1968.

[83] Dr. Sheldon Kushner, interview, July 2013.

[84] Gas gangrene is the "death and decay of wound tissue infected by the soil bacterium clostridium per-fringens. Toxins produced by the bacterium cause putrefactive decay to connective tissue with the generation of gas. Gas gangrene is marked by a high fever, brownish pus, gas bubbles under the skin, skin discoloration, and a foul odor." ("Gas gangrene," Enclyclopedia.com, www.encyclopedia.com/caregiving/dictionaries-thesauruses-pictures-and-press-releases/gas-gangrene).

[85] Dr. Sheldon Kushner, interview, August 2015.

[86] Back of photograph from Dr. Sheldon Kushner, July 1968.

[87] Dr. Sheldon Kushner, interview, August 2015.

[88] The Ascaris worm is a nematode worm that gains access to the intestine through ingestion of Ascaris eggs in feces in unsanitary areas, such as the Mekong River (from Encyclopedia.com and conversation with Dr. Sheldon Kushner, November 2016).

[89] Dr. Sheldon Kushner, interview, November 2016.

[90] Tetanus is an infection of the nervous system that comes from the potentially deadly bacteria that live in the soil and are found around the world. While the spore form can remain inactive in the soil, it can remain infectious for more than 40 years. Infection starts when the spores enter the body through an injury or wound. The spores release bacteria that spread and make a poison called tetanospasmin. This poison blocks nerve signals from the spinal cord to the muscles, causing severe muscle spasms. The spasms can be so powerful that they tear the muscles or cause fractures of the spine. The time between infection and the first sign of symptoms is typically 7 to 21 days (see "About Tetanus," Centers for Disease Control and Prevention, www.cdc.gov/tetanus/about/, and "Tetanus: Symptoms, Causes, and Treatments," Medical News Today, www.medicalnewstoday.com/articles/163063.php.

[91] Dr. Sheldon Kushner, letter, September 20, 1968.

[92] Wilensky, Robert J. Military Medicine to Win Hearts and Minds, Texas Tech Univerisity Press, 2004, p. 70.

[93] Dr. Sheldon Kushner, letter, May 24, 1968.

[94] Dr. Sheldon Kushner, interview November 2014.

[95] Dr. Sheldon Kushner, interview, November 2014.

[96] Dr. Sheldon Kushner, interview, July 2013.

[97] Tom Graue, interview, June 2012.

[98] A craniotomy is the surgical removal of part of the bone from the skull to expose the brain (see "Craniotomy," Johns Hopkins Medicine, www.hopkinsmedicine.org/healthlibrary/test_procedures/neurological/craniotomy_92,P08767/).

[99] Ibid.

[100] Heparin, sometimes misspelled *Heprin*, is an anticoagulant used to treat and prevent blood clots in the veins, arteries, or lungs. It is also used before surgery to reduce the risk of blood clot (see "Heparin," Drugs.com, www.drugs.com/heparin.html).

[101] Dextran is used to treat hypovolemia (a decrease in the volume of circulating blood plasma) that can result from severe blood loss after surgery, injuries such as severe burns, or other causes of bleeding (see "Dextran," Drugs.com, www.drugs.com/mtm/dextran-high-molecular-weight.html).

[102] Dr. Sheldon Kushner, interview, November 2014.

[103] Macrodex is a high-molecular weight dextran plasma volume expander derived from natural sources of sugar (glucose). It works by restoring blood plasma lost through severe bleeding. Severe blood loss can decrease oxygen levels, which can lead to organ failure, brain damage, coma, and possibly death. Plasma is needed to circulate red blood cells that deliver oxygen throughout the body (see "Dextran," Drugs.com, www.drugs.com/mtm/dextran-high-molecular-weight.html)

[104] Dr. Sheldon Kushner, tape recording, October 20, 1968.

[105] Debridement is the medical removal of dead, damaged, or contaminated (infected) tissue to improve the healing potential of the remaining tissue (see "Debridement," Merriam-Webster, www.merriam-webster.com/dictionary/debridement).

[106] Occasionally, wounds are closed by delayed primary closure; patients undergo irrigation of a wound and debridement until wounds appear clean to close inspection, at which time they are closed completely. The benefit of delayed primary closure is related to improved blood flow at the wound edges, which develops increasingly over the first few days (see "Experience with Wound VAC and Delayed Primary Closure of Contaminated Soft Tissue Injuries in Iraq," *Journal of Trauma and Acute Care Surgery* 61, no. 5 (November 2006), journals.lww.com/jtrauma/Abstract/2006/11000/Experience_With_Wound_VAC_and_Delayed_Primary.27.aspx) .

[107] Dr. Sheldon Kushner, interview, November 2014.

[108] Dr. Sheldon Kushner, interview, November 2014.

[109] Dr. Sheldon Kushner, interview, November 2014.

[110] Dr. Sheldon Kushner, interview, October 2012.

[111] Ibid.

[112] Ibid.

[113] Ibid.

[114] Ibid.

[115] Dr. Sheldon Kushner, tape recording, April 1, 1968.

[116] Dr. Sheldon Kushner, tape recording, August 2, 1968.

[117] Dr. Sheldon Kushner, letter, September 8, 1968.

[118] Dr. Sheldon Kushner, letter, October 28, 1968.

[119] Dr. Sheldon Kushner, interview, November 2016.

[120] Dr. Sheldon Kushner, letter, January 11, 1969.

[121] Dr. Sheldon Kushner, letter, January 31, 1969.

122 Dr. Sheldon Kushner, letter, May 13, 1968.

123 Dr. Sheldon Kushner, letter, May 23, 1968.

124 Dr. Sheldon Kushner, letter, April 10, 1968.

125 Dr. Sheldon Kushner, letter, June 18, 1968.

126 Dr. Sheldon Kushner, email to the author, April 12, 2017.

127 Dr. Sheldon Kushner, letter, November 3, 1968.

128 Dr. Sheldon Kushner, tape recording, April 1, 1968.

129 Dr. Sheldon Kushner, letter, April 9, 1969.

130 Dr. Sheldon Kushner, letter, May 17, 1968.

131 Dr. Sheldon Kushner, letter, May 5, 1968.

132 Dr. Sheldon Kushner, letter, May 6, 1968.

133 Dr. Sheldon Kushner, letter, May 12, 1968.

134 Dr. Sheldon Kushner, letter, May 13, 1968.

135 Dr. Sheldon Kushner, letter, May 16, 1968.

136 Dr. Sheldon Kushner, letter, June 10, 1968.

137 Dr. Sheldon Kushner, tape recording, June 16, 1968.

138 Dr. Sheldon Kushner, letter, June 23, 1968.

139 Dr. Sheldon Kushner, letter, July 16, 1968.

140 Dr. Sheldon Kushner, letter, July 18, 1968.

141 Dr. Sheldon Kushner, letter, July 22, 1968.

142 Dr. Sheldon Kushner, letter, July 24, 1968.

143 Dr. Sheldon Kushner, letter, July 31, 1968.

144 Dr. Sheldon Kushner, tape recording, August 2, 1968.

145 Dr. Sheldon Kushner, letter, August 19, 1968.

146 Dr. Sheldon Kushner, letter, August 26, 1968.

147 Dr. Sheldon Kushner, letter, August 27, 1968.

148 Dr. Sheldon Kushner, letter, August 28, 1968.

149 Dr. Sheldon Kushner, tape recording, September 1968.

150 Dr. Sheldon Kushner, letter, September 13, 1968.

151 Dr. Sheldon Kushner, letter, October 30, 1968.

152 Dr. Sheldon Kushner, letter, November 1, 1968.

153 Dr. Sheldon Kushner, letter, November 3, 1968.

154 Dr. Sheldon Kushner, letter, November 16, 1968.

155 Dr. Sheldon Kushner, letter, December 11, 1968.

156 Dr. Sheldon Kushner, letter, December 28, 1968.

157 Dr. Sheldon Kushner, letter, December 23, 1968.

158 Dr. Sheldon Kushner, letter, January 2, 1969.

159 Dr. Sheldon Kushner, letter, January 18, 1969.

160 Dr. Sheldon Kushner, letter, February 15, 1969.

1661 Dr. Sheldon Kushner, letter, February 17, 1969.

162 Dr. Sheldon Kushner, letter, February 23, 1969.

163 Dr. Sheldon Kushner, interview, July 2013.

[164] Dr. Sheldon Kushner, interview, November 2014.

[165] Dr. Sheldon Kushner, letter, May 1, 1968.

[166] Dr. Sheldon Kushner, letter, July 25, 1968.

[167] Dr. Sheldon Kushner, letter, August 31, 1968.

[168] Dr. Sheldon Kushner, tape recording, August 2, 1968.

[169] Dr. Sheldon Kushner interview November 2016.

[170] Dr. Sheldon Kushner, letter, December 20, 1968.

[171] Dr. Sheldon Kushner, letter, June 20, 1968.

[172] Dr. Sheldon Kushner, letter, February 17, 1969.

[173] Dr. Sheldon Kushner, letter, September 1, 1968.

[174] Dr. Sheldon Kushner, letter, January 11, 1969.

[175] Dr. Sheldon Kushner, interview, August 2016.

[176] Dr. Sheldon Kushner, letter, March 2, 1969.

[177] Dr. Sheldon Kushner, interview, November 2014.

[178] Ibid.

[179] Ibid.

[180] Dr. Sheldon Kushner, interview, August 2015.

[181] Dr. Sheldon Kushner, interview, December 2016.

[182] The Kent State shootings (also known as the May 4 massacre or the Kent State massacre) occurred at Kent State University in the Kent, Ohio, and involved the shooting of unarmed college students by the Ohio National Guard on Monday, May 4, 1970. The guardsmen fired 67 rounds over a period of 13 seconds, killing four students and wounding nine others, one of whom suffered permanent paralysis (see Jerry M. Lewis and Thomas R. Hensley, "The May 4 Shootings at Kent State University: The Search for Historical Accuracy," Kent State University, www.kent.edu/may-4-historical-accuracy, and "Kent State Shootings," Ohio History Central, www.ohiohistorycentral.org/w/Kent_State_Shootings).

[183] Post-traumatic stress disorder, or PTSD, is a mental health condition that is triggered by a terrifying event—either experiencing it or witnessing it. Symptoms may include flashbacks, nightmares, and severe anxiety, as well as uncontrollable thoughts about the event (see "Post-traumatic Stress Disorder (PTSD)," Mayo Clinic, www.mayoclinic.org/diseases-conditions/post-traumatic-stress-disorder/home/ovc-20308548).

[184] Dr. Sheldon Kushner, interview, July 2013.

[185] As of this writing, Andrea Kushner is an attorney in California and David Kushner is a social worker in Ocala, Florida.

[186] Dr. Sheldon Kushner, interview, August 2015.

[187] Dr. Sheldon Kushner, interview, November 2016.

[188] Dr. Sheldon Kushner, interview, November 2014.

[189] Dr. Sheldon Kushner, tape recording, September 1968.

[190] Dr. Sheldon Kushner, interview, November 2014.

[191] Ibid.

[192] Tom Graue, interview, June 2012.

[193] Dr. Sheldon Kushner, letter, May 15,1968.

[194] Dr. Sheldon Kushner, letter, July 6, 1968.

[195] Dr. Sheldon Kushner, letter, August 8, 1968.

[196] USS *Pueblo*: On January 23, 1968, the USS *Pueblo*, a Navy intelligence vessel with 83 crew members, was "engaged in a routine surveillance of the North Korean coast when it was intercepted by North Korean patrol boats. According to U.S. reports, the *Pueblo* was in international waters almost 16 miles from shore, but the North Koreans turned their guns on the lightly armed vessel and demanded its surrender. The Americans attempted to escape, and the North Koreans opened fire, wounding the commander and two others. With capture inevitable, the Americans stalled for time, destroying the classified information aboard while taking further fire. Several more crew members were wounded." The event came less than a week after President Lyndon B. Johnson's State of the Union address to the U.S. Congress, just a week before the start of the Tet Offensive in South Vietnam during the Vietnam War (see "USS Pueblo Captured," History.com, www.history.com/this-day-in-history/uss-pueblo-captured).

[197] Dr. Sheldon Kushner, letter, December 20, 1968.

[198] Dr. Sheldon Kushner, interview, November 2014.

[199] Ibid.

[200] Dr. Sheldon Kushner, interview, November 2014.

[201] Dr. Sheldon Kushner, interview, November 2014.

[202] Colonel David Haskell Hackworth (November 11, 1930–May 4, 2005), also known as "Hack," was an Korean War and Vietnam War veteran who received many combat decorations for heroism in both wars.

[203] Sheldon's letter can be found online at www.hackworth.com/vgrunts.html.

About the Author

Mary Jane Ingui, PhD.

*Mary has a Ph.D. from Lehigh University and has taught
at the college level for years. In addition, she has been a newspaper
correspondent, which drew her into a keen interest in the stories of veterans,
such as Dr. Kushner. Mary has many academic articles to her credit,
and has written extensively about Italian-American women
in the 20th century.*

78463764R00110

Made in the USA
Columbia, SC
17 October 2017